Weather

Weather

Louis J. Battan

University of Arizona

Prentice-Hall, Inc.,   Englewood Cliffs, New Jersey

Library of Congress Cataloging in Publication Data

BATTAN, LOUIS J.
   Weather.

   (Foundations of earth science series)
   Bibliography: p. 133
   1. Weather.
QC981.B33   551.6   73-17080
ISBN   0-13-947770-5
ISBN   0-13-947762-4 (pbk.)

FOUNDATIONS OF EARTH SCIENCE SERIES

A. Lee McAlester, Editor

Illustrations by Richard Kassouf

10   9   8   7   6   5   4   3   2   1

PRENTICE-HALL INTERNATIONAL, INC., *London*
PRENTICE-HALL OF AUSTRALIA, PTY. LTD., *Sydney*
PRENTICE-HALL OF CANADA, LTD., *Toronto*
PRENTICE-HALL OF INDIA PRIVATE LIMITED, *New Delhi*
PRENTICE-HALL OF JAPAN, INC., *Tokyo*

Foundations
of Earth Science Series

Elementary Earth Science textbooks have too long reflected mere traditions in teaching rather than the triumphs and uncertainties of present-day science. In geology, the time-honored textbook emphasis on geomorphic processes and descriptive stratigraphy, a pattern begun by James Dwight Dana over a century ago, is increasingly anachronistic in an age of shifting research frontiers and disappearing boundaries between long-established disciplines. At the same time, the extraordinary expansions in exploration of the oceans, atmosphere, and interplanetary space within the past decade have made obsolete the unnatural separation of the "solid Earth" science of geology from the "fluid Earth" sciences of oceanography, meteorology, and planetary astronomy, and have emphasized the need for authorative introductory textbooks in these vigorous subjects.

Stemming from the conviction that beginning students deserve to share in the excitement of modern research, the *Foundations of Earth Science Series* has been planned to provide brief, readable, up-to-date introductions to all aspects of modern Earth science. Each volume has been written by an authority on the subject covered, thus insuring a first-hand treatment seldom found in introductory textbooks. Four of the volumes—*Structure of the Earth, Earth Materials, The Surface of the Earth,* and *Earth Resources*— cover topics traditionally taught in physical geology courses. Four more volumes—*Geologic Time, Ancient Environments, The History of the Earth's Crust,* and *The History of Life*—treat historical topics. The remaining volumes—*Oceans, Man and the Ocean, Atmospheres, Weather,* and *The Solar System*—deal with the "fluid Earth" sciences of oceanography and atmospheric and planetary sciences. Each volume, however, is complete in itself and can be combined with other volumes in any sequence, thus allowing the teacher great flexibility in course arrangement. In addition, these compact and inexpensive volumes can be used individually to supplement and enrich other introductory textbooks.

Contents

1

General features of

the Earth's atmosphere

The Earth is unique in many ways. None of the other planets of the solar system has its vast oceans and none has an atmosphere similar in composition to that of the Earth. Other books in this series have discussed planetary atmospheres and the oceans.* In this small book, we intend to examine the Earth's atmosphere, its properties and behavior, the formation of clouds and storms, the factors governing its climates, how future weather is predicted, and how the weather may be changed or controlled.

Composition of Clean Air

The atmosphere is a mixture of gases and aerosols, the latter being the name given to small solid and liquid particles distributed in the air. Aerosols will be discussed later; at this time, we shall consider only the atmospheric gases.

*K. K. Turekian, *Oceans*, Prentice-Hall, 1968; B. J. Skinner and K. K Turekian, *Man and the Ocean*, Prentice-Hall, 1973; R. M. Goody and J. C. G. Walker, *Atmospheres*, Prentice-Hall, 1972.

The term *air* is commonly used as if it were a specific gas, but that is not in fact the case. Air is a mixture of many gases; some are considered to be a permanent part of the atmosphere because they remain in fixed proportion to the total gas volume. Other gases vary a great deal in time and space. When the air is dry, that is, when there is no water vapor in it, the relative concentrations of various gases in the atmosphere are as shown in Table 1–1. These quantities are essentially constant all over the Earth and do not change up to an altitude of about 80 km.

Table 1–1

Principal Gases Composing the Earth's Atmosphere

Constituent	Percent by Volume of Dry Air	Concentration in Parts per Million (ppm) of Air
Nitrogen (N_2)	78.084	
Oxygen (O_2)	20.946	
Argon (A)	0.934	
Neon (Ne)	0.00182	18.2
Helium (He)	0.000524	5.24
Methane (CH_4)	0.00015	1.5
Krypton (Kr)	0.000114	1.14
Hydrogen (H_2)	0.00005	0.5
Important variable gases		
Water vapor (H_2O)	0–3	
Carbon dioxide (CO_2)°	0.0325	325
Carbon monoxide (CO)		< 100
Sulfur dioxide (SO_2)		0–1
Nitrogen dioxide (NO_2)		0–0.2
Ozone (O_3)		0–2

*Carbon dioxide is uniformly mixed through the atmosphere but is increasing at a rate of about 0.7 ppm per year. Its concentration was about 325 ppm in 1974.

Of the two principal constituents, nitrogen is a relatively inert gas which reacts with other substances only under unusual circumstances and therefore its concentration in the atmosphere remains essentially constant.

On the other hand, it has been suggested that the oxygen content in the Earth's atmosphere is continually decreasing as a result of two factors, a reduction of the plant life which converts carbon dioxide to oxygen and the burning of fossil fuels. There is no evidence that this has happened or is likely to happen in the foreseeable future. Measurements of oxygen content indicate no change over this century and no measurable changes are projected into the distant future. There is a virtual balance between photosynthetic production of oxygen and its utilization by animals and bacteria.

Some of the highly variable minor gases in the atmosphere are very important ones. Many gaseous pollutants, to be discussed later, fall into this category. A most important gas from the human point of view is ozone. It is composed of three atoms of oxygen and has the symbol O_3. There is very little ozone in the atmosphere, less than about 0.00005 percent by volume. Near the ground, in certain large cities such as Los Angeles, ozone may attain concentrations as high as 0.1 ppm* in extreme cases, but most of the ozone appears in the altitude layer 10 to 50 km above the ground. Between the levels of 20 and 30 km ozone concentrations often amount to 0.1 to 0.2 ppm.

The ozone layer is not constant. It varies with altitude, latitude, season of the year and time of day. The ozone is formed by photochemical reactions. Oxygen molecules (O_2) absorbing shortwave solar radiation are dissociated to form oxygen atoms (O). Collisions of oxygen molecules, atoms, and other particles lead to the formation of ozone (O_3). It, in turn, strongly absorbs ultraviolet radiation from the sun which ionizes the ozone to produce O and O_2. There are many other chemical reactions involved in the formation and distribution of ozone. Theoretical studies have indicated the rates at which the appropriate processes must occur to account for the observed distribution of ozone in the upper atmosphere.

It is fortunate that the ozone layer exists to absorb ultraviolet radiation. If it did not, the radiation could produce harmful biological effects on Earth. Sunburns would be more severe and skin cancers would be much more common. This fact has been used by certain scientists in opposing the development of high-flying supersonic transport airplanes. The engines of such aircraft emit nitrogen oxides which may react with and reduce the concentrations of ozone at the flight altitudes of about 20 km. If this occurred, more ultraviolet radiation would reach the Earth and there would be more skin cancers. This claim has not been verified, but it is worthy of attention.

One of the most vital and highly variable gases in the atmosphere is water vapor. In a dry desert region it may be present in barely measurable amounts. At the other extreme, in warm, saturated air at sea level, it may account for 3 percent of the volume of air. When the air contains water vapor it is said to be moist air. Sometimes the term "moisture in the air" is used to designate not only the quantity of gaseous H_2O but also of the liquid droplets of H_2O constituting a cloud. In this discussion of the atmosphere's composition, only the water vapor is being considered. It should be noted, however, that for the atmosphere as a whole the quantity of H_2O in the form of liquid or water cloud particles is small with respect to the gaseous H_2O in the atmosphere.

*The symbol ppm stands for parts per million, a unit used to express small fractional quantities of one substance in a quantity of another substance. For example, 0.1 ppm by volume represents a volume of 0.1 cm^3 of ozone in 10^6 cm^3 of air.

There are many ways to express the degree of moisture in the air, and as a result confusion sometimes arises as to their precise meanings. For example, two common terms are *absolute humidity* and *relative humidity*. The former is the mass of water vapor in a unit volume of air; this is the same as the density of the water vapor in the air. The latter can be determined with sufficient accuracy by taking the ratio, expressed in percent, of the absolute humidity of the air at a given temperature to the absolute humidity the air would have if it were saturated with water vapor at the same temperature. More will be said about this in a later chapter.

Another common gas in the Earth's atmosphere is carbon dioxide. Although its concentration is fairly uniform over the Earth, it has been rising steadily for the last century or so (see Fig. 1–1). Since 1960 the concentra-

FIGURE 1–1 *Calculations of carbon dioxide concentrations added to the Earth's atmosphere by the combustion of fossil fuels. From L. Machta,* Brookhaven Symposium, May, 1972.

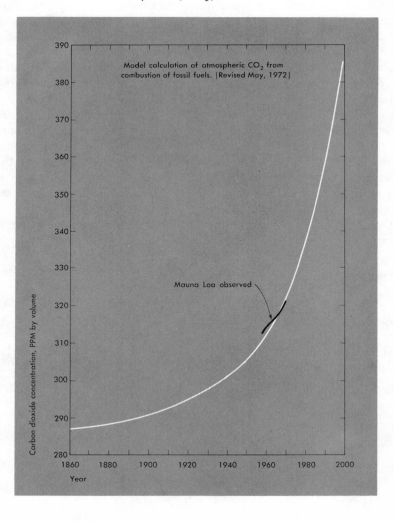

tion of CO_2 has been increasing at a rate of about 0.7 ppm per year. This increase is attributed largely to the burning of fossil fuels—coal, oil, gas. It has been estimated that about half of the CO_2 put into the atmosphere by fossil fuel combustion has remained there. The remainder is taken up by vegetation and absorbed by the oceans. Assuming rates of fuel consumption and exchange rates, it has been estimated that by the year 2000, CO_2 concentrations in the atmosphere will reach a level of about 380 ppm. This would represent an increase of about 18 percent above the 322 ppm observed in 1970.

The interest in carbon dioxide has not been based on any concern about its toxic consequences. Instead, carbon dioxide has been getting a great deal of attention because it is a good absorber of infrared radiation, and therefore it influences energy transfers through the atmosphere. In general, if it were acting alone in a static atmosphere, an increase of carbon dioxide would lead to a warming of the lower atmosphere. It is well known, however, that the atmosphere is not a simple static system, and hence the overall results of the increases of CO_2 are not easily estimated. Nevertheless, they must be taken into account when evaluating the effects of gases and aerosols on worldwide temperatures. This matter will be discussed in more detail in a later chapter.

Pollutants in the Atmosphere

In a sense carbon dioxide might be considered a pollutant because its concentration is being increased by human activity and its consequences ultmimately may be harmful. On the other hand, it does not pose the direct and immediate threat to humans, animals, vegetation, and property as do certain other well-known gases and particles.

One of the best known atmospheric contaminants is sulfur dioxide (SO_2). It gets into the air mostly through the burning of coal and oil and as a result of the smelting of sulfur-bearing minerals. Power plants, oil refineries, and copper smelters are prolific emitters of SO_2. In the vicinity of such places, concentrations may be many parts per million, and reach levels which damage vegetation and, given the appropriate meteorological conditions, can be lethal to people and animals. In large cities the concentrations of SO_2 seldom exceed 1 ppm, but even this low level is regarded as dangerously high to very young and very old people, particularly those with respiratory problems.

One of the points to remember when considering pollutants such as SO_2 is that they seldom exist alone; the various gases and particles are mixed together. In the presence of water vapor and sunlight, they may react and combine to produce substances more harmful than any of the existing gases or particles taken alone.

Sulfur dioxide gas in the presence of sufficient water vapor becomes sulfur trioxide SO_3 and ultimately tiny particles of H_2SO_4, sulfuric acid. This substance can cause serious damage when deposited in the lung. It can also cause vegetation and many solid materials such as textiles, paper, and leather to deteriorate.

Nitrogen dioxide (NO_2) is formed by the fixation of nitrogen and oxygen in a combustion process at high temperatures such as occurs in an automobile engine. This gas can be toxic in sufficient concentrations. Fortunately, even in Los Angeles with its high density of automobiles and freeways, the quantities of NO_2 seldom exceed 0.1 to 0.2 ppm.

Motor vehicles also produce large quantities of the well-known gas carbon monoxide (CO). Unlike carbon dioxide, it attacks the hemoglobin in the blood and prevents it from transporting oxygen from the lungs to the tissues of the body. The concentration of CO may be as high as 100 ppm for brief periods during the peak travel times in a large city. It is highly variable depending on traffic and atmospheric conditions and is regarded as a dangerous air pollutant. Concentrations of carbon monoxide of 10 ppm or more for a period of 8 hours can slow down human responses.

Still another undesirable class of gases put into the atmosphere mostly by automobiles, trucks, and airplanes is composed of hydrocarbons. They are vaporized components of unburned petroleum fuel. Concentrations usually are less than 1 to 2 ppm, but hydrocarbons contribute to a great deal of human discomfort. They react with nitrogen oxides, ozone, and other substances in the presence of sunlight and produce the photochemical smog which causes the eye irritation so familiar in the Los Angeles area.

Aerosols

The atmosphere contains huge numbers of solids and liquid particles. The largest ones associated with clouds, rain, snow, and hail will be discussed in a later chapter. At this time consider only the small ones most of which are invisible to the unaided eye. Most of the particles are composed of the following: soil blown into the air; salts remaining when droplets of ocean water dry out; smoke from combustion processes; various substances thrown into the atmosphere by volcanoes; sulfate and nitrate particles produced by chemical processes in the atmosphere; and tiny droplets of sulfuric or nitric acid formed in the air.

The presence of aerosols can be detected in a number of ways. The particles can be captured on slides and viewed by means of an optical or electron microscope. In some instances, chemical spot tests can be employed to identify their chemical compositions. The concentration of particles can be measured with an Aitken nuclei counter. This device consists of a chamber which takes a sample of air and expands it rapidly. As a result of the expansion, the air is cooled suddenly and, for reasons to be discussed in Chapter 5, water vapor condenses on the particles and a cloud is formed. By measuring the opacity of the resulting cloud, it is possible to estimate the concentration of particles which were present in the air and had radii greater than about 10^{-3} microns.

An estimate of the particulate loading, that is, the mass of particles in a unit volume of air, can be obtained by means of filters through which a large volume of air is passed. The filter is weighed before and after the sample is taken to determine the mass of particles. Certain chemical tests allow evaluation of the relative amounts of particular substances, but these schemes give almost no information about the sizes of the particles.

The overall particulate loading of the atmosphere also can be estimated by optical techniques. For example, measurements of the changes in incoming solar radiation on cloudless days can be related to atmospheric turbidity. The backscattering of light from an intense searchlight beam or better still from a laser beam pointing upwards at night, can be used to locate a layer of particles and estimate their sizes and concentration.

Table 1–2 presents some data on the concentrations of particles observed

Table 1–2

Concentration of Aitken Particles in the Atmosphere

Location	Number of Measurements	Concentrations (particles cm^{-3})		
		Average	Minimum	Maximum
Ocean	600	940	2	39,800
Mountain				
Above 2 km	190	950	6	27,000
1–2 km	1,000	2,130	0	37,000
0.5–1 km	870	6,000	30	155,000
Country, inland	3,500	9,500	180	336,000
Town	4,700	34,300	620	400,000
City	2,500	147,000	3,500	4,000,000

Source: H. Landsberg, Atmospheric condensation nuclei. *Ergebn. Kosm. Phys.*, 1938.

in the atmosphere by means of an Aitken nuclei counter. The table shows that over continents, particularly in urban areas, the particle concentrations are very much higher than over the oceans. In the atmosphere, the smaller the particles the greater the number. Particles having radii of 10^{-5} cm may occur in concentrations of about 10^4 cm^{-3} while those of radii 10^{-3} cm may be as few as 10^{-2} cm^{-1}.

The average residence time of particles in the atmosphere depends on where they are located. Those in the lower atmosphere remain in the air only one to four weeks. Tiny particles thrown into the stratosphere, above about 10 km, by volcanic eruptions may stay there for a year or two. The absence of clouds and rain in the stratosphere and the small fall velocities of the particles, account for these long periods.

There is no doubt that over many large and growing cities, the aerosol concentrations have increased over the last few decades. A crucial question, still not satisfactorily answered, is concerned with the degree to which human activity is increasing the average level of particulates in the whole atmosphere. Since they interfere with the transfer of radiant energy through the atmosphere a significant increase in the aerosol content might have an important effect on the global climate.

The available evidence indicates that there has been an increase of aerosols over the Northern Hemisphere but little change over the Southern Hemisphere. Figure 1–2 shows a curve of atmospheric turbidity based on data collected on a mountain top in Hawaii. The greater the turbidity, the greater the quantity of particles in the air. These observations clearly show the injection of particles into the atmosphere by several major volcanoes.

FIGURE 1–2 *Departure from normal of atmospheric turbidity measurements over Tucson, Arizona and Mauna Loa, Hawaii. The curves are based on average yearly values. From K. Heidel, Science, 1972, 177: 882–883.*

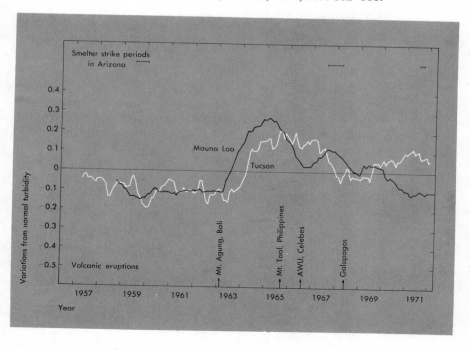

Following the massive eruptions of Krakatoa in 1883 and Mount Agung in 1963, sunsets were particularly brilliant and colorful for most of the succeeding two years. The minute particles scattered the blue colors of sunlight more than the red and led to magnificent skies at sunrise and sunset.

After about 1963, there were no really massive volcanic explosions, and the turbidity level returned to close to its value of earlier years. Measurements of the particulate fallout on the glaciers in the Soviet Union have suggested an increase of atmospheric loading. Other evidence could be cited to show that the evidence on the world-wide particulate pollution is conflicting. We shall return to this topic in Chapter 7.

Radiation

Even a casual view of weather systems such as hurricanes indicates that large amounts of energy are involved. In order to account for the wind currents over the earth, the energy requirements become enormous. Where does the energy come from, how is it transferred from place to place, how do the gases and aerosols influence energy transfer, and how is it converted from one form of energy to another? These are among the central questions in meteorology.

In the atmosphere, heat is transferred by three methods—conduction, convection, and radiation. As everyone knows, conduction occurs by the direct transfer of heat from one substance to another in contact with it. If you touch a hot object, your hand becomes hot as heat is conducted to it.

Convection transfers heat by means of mass motions of the medium. When warm air rises and cool air sinks, heat is transported upwards in the atmosphere. Similarly, when warm air moves poleward and cool air moves equatorward, there is a transfer of heat towards the pole. This form of horizontal convection is called *advection* by meteorologists. Both convection and advection play crucial roles in atmospheric heat transfer, but for the earth as a whole advection is most important because of the very large masses of air involved.

The mechanism of heat transfer in the atmosphere which will be examined in some detail at this time is radiation. It involves the transfer of energy by means of electromagnetic waves and is effective even when there is not a material substance involved. Radiant energy can pass through a vacuum such as outer space. It can also pass through various media but with a certain degree of interference. For example, some types of radiation are partially absorbed by water vapor and carbon dioxide and hence cannot pass readily through the atmosphere.

In order to understand the behavior of the atmosphere, it is essential to know something about the nature of radiation. Everyone is familiar with

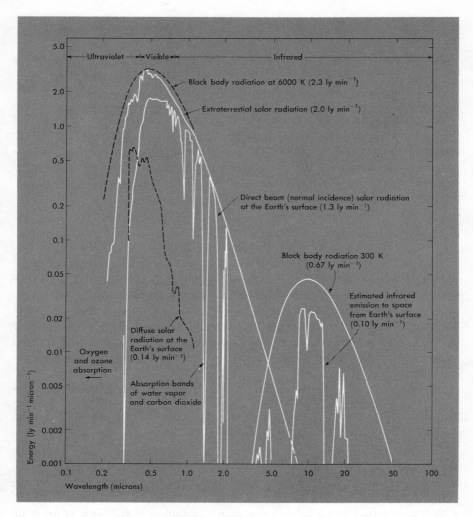

FIGURE 1–3   *Spectra of solar and terrestrial radiation. The blackbody radiation at 6,000°K is reduced by the square of the ratio of the Sun's radius to the average distance between the Sun and the Earth in order to give the energy flux that would be incident on the top of the Earth's atmosphere. From W. D. Sellers,* Physical Climatology, *University of Chicago Press, 1965.*

certain aspects of radiation from the Sun. It warms the Earth and gives you a sunburn if you expose yourself too long. Sometimes during a summer shower, you see a rainbow which shows that sunlight is composed of many colors from violet to red. Since each of the colors corresponds to a particular wavelength of the electromagnetic spectrum, you would suspect that the Sun also emits energy at wavelengths other than the visible. (See Fig. 1–3.)

General features of the Earth's atmosphere

Most of the energy radiated from a very hot body such as the Sun is in the form of very short electromagnetic waves. Almost all the energy falls in the wavelength interval from close to zero up to perhaps 4 or 5 microns. The peak emissions are in the visible wavelengths from violet at about 0.4 micron to red at about 0.7 micron. Sometimes these wavelengths are expressed in Angstrom units (abbreviated Å); violet and red correspond to wavelengths of about 4,000 and 7,000 Å respectively.

Radiant energies at wavelengths shorter than violet are said to be in the ultraviolet band and cannot be seen, but they can be absorbed effectively by ozone. This absorption accounts for a warm layer of air in the high atmosphere at altitudes where ozone is found. At still shorter wavelengths in the solar spectrum, one encounters X rays.

Wavelengths longer than those of visible red waves are called infrared. They may range in length from just over 0.7 micron to perhaps 100 microns. A relatively cool body such as the Earth emits maximum radiant energy at wavelengths of 10 to 15 microns.

It is a physical fact that every substance—gas, liquid or solid—radiates energy unless its temperature could be reduced to absolute zero. The quantity of the radiation and its spectral properties depends on the characteristics of the substance, particularly its temperature. The maximum amount of radiation at a given temperature is called the *blackbody radiation,* a phrase that may be misleading because a substance nearly having this property might not be black or might not be a body. At any rate, if any object such as the Sun or the Earth behaves as a blackbody, its radiation spectrum can be calculated from the temperature. Several well-known radiation laws make this possible. The Stefan-Boltzmann Law states that the total emissive power of a body is proportional to the fourth power of the absolute temperature. Planck's Law specifies how the emission of a blackbody varies with wavelength at any particular temperature.

When considering the radiation from any substance, it is necessary to recognize that they do not radiate exactly as black bodies. This fact is taken into account by specifying a property called the *emissivity.* It is the ratio of the actual emitted power to that which would be emitted by a blackbody at the same temperature.

Radiation falling on any substance can undergo various processes. It can be absorbed in whole or part and be used to warm up the absorbing substance. Also, part of the radiation can be reflected or *scattered,* a word commonly used by physicists. The term reflected implies that the radiation is redirected backward, whereas in reality, it can be scattered in all directions—backward, sideways, and forward.

Figure 1–3 presents spectra of solar and terrestrial radiation at representative temperatures of the Sun and Earth. The smooth curves are those which would correspond to blackbodies. The irregular curves show the ef-

General features of the Earth's atmosphere

fects of gases, particles, and nonblackbody emission in the atmosphere. More will be said about these points in the discussion to follow.

Heat Balance of the Atmosphere

The average atmospheric temperature of the Earth varies slowly. Over a period of half a century the average air temperature near the surface may increase or decrease by one degree Celsius. From certain points of view such a change is very important. It can have a profound effect on sea ice, sea level and the growing season in marginal regions of the world. Nevertheless, when considering the overall heat balance of the Earth it is reasonable to begin with the assumption that the temperature is constant over a long period. In order for this to be true the amount of incoming solar radiation must be balanced by the amount of outgoing radiation from the surface of the Earth and the atmosphere.

The average rate of incoming radiation falling on the outer limit of the atmosphere at normal incidence is called the *solar constant*. Its value is taken to be about 2.0 langleys per minute where one langley (abbreviated ly) equals one calorie per square centimeter. If this quantity is multiplied by the surface area of the Earth, the total solar energy intercepted is about 3.67×10^{21} cal day^{-1}. If it were distributed uniformly over the surface of the globe, the amount received per unit of area would be 263 kilolangleys per year (abbreviated kly yr^{-1}). Of course the energy is not uniform over the Earth; the areas near the equator get about 2.4 times more solar radiation than those near the poles.

Incidentally, other sources of energy for the atmosphere such as heat from the interior of the Earth, reflections of solar energy or radiation from the moon, and energy from the solar tides are much smaller than the sun's direct insolation. In total they are about 0.0002 of the solar constant, and therefore they can be disregarded when considering the energy budget of the global atmosphere.

The magnitude of the total incoming solar radiation is related to the total energies of various other phenomena and processes as seen in Table 1–3. It is evident that most items in the list expend very small quantities of energy in comparison to the total solar radiation incident on the top of the atmosphere. The table also shows that most human endeavors such as the generation of power at Hoover Dam and the explosion of nuclear weapons involve quantities of energy which are small in comparison with the energy from the Sun. In later chapters we shall discuss most of the weather phenomena listed. The table gives a scale for judging the energetics of each one. For example, it can be seen that a lightning stroke represents only about 0.00001 of the energy in an average summer thunderstorm.

General features of the Earth's atmosphere

Table 1–3

Approximate Total Energies of Geophysical Phenomena and Human Activities Related to the Total Solar Energy Intercepted by the Earth—3.67 x 10^{21} Calories per Day

Solar energy received by the Earth per day	1
World use of energy in 1950	10^{-2}
Strong earthquake	10^{-2}
Average cyclone	10^{-3}
Average hurricane	10^{-4}
Eruption of Krakatoa volcano, August, 1883	10^{-5}
Detonation of "thermonuclear weapon" in April, 1965	10^{-5}
Kinetic energy of the general circulation	10^{-5}
Average squall line	10^{-6}
Average magnetic storm	10^{-7}
Average summer thunderstorm	10^{-8}
Detonation of 20 kiloton Nagasaki bomb, August, 1945	10^{-8}
Average earthquake	10^{-8}
Burning of 7,000 tons of coal	10^{-8}
Daily output of Hoover Dam	10^{-8}
Average forest fire in the United States, 1952–53	10^{-9}
Average local shower	10^{-10}
Average tornado	10^{-11}
Street lighting on average night in New York City	10^{-11}
Average lightning stroke	10^{-13}
Individual gust of air near the Earth's surface	10^{-17}
Meteorite	10^{-18}

Source: W. D. Sellers, *Physical Climatology*, University of Chicago Press, 1965.

A substantial fraction of the solar energy incident on the top of the atmosphere is reflected back to outer space by clouds, other aerosols and air molecules. The fraction is called the Earth's albedo, and on the average is about 0.36. Before weather satellites came into regular use, estimates of the albedo were based on inadequate global observations, and the widely used values were too high.

Consider what happens to the 263 kly yr^{-1} of insolation assumed to be uniformly received over the surface of the earth at the outer limits of the atmosphere. As illustrated in Fig. 1–4, 36 percent, or 94 kly yr^{-1}, are reflected back by clouds and atmosphere. Atmospheric gases, dust, and clouds absorb 45 kly yr^{-1}, the surface of the Earth absorbs 124 kly yr^{-1}, and 16 kly yr^{-1} are reflected from the Earth's surface.

In order to prevent a steady warming or cooling of the Earth, the 169 kly yr^{-1} of energy absorbed by the atmosphere, the land, and the water of

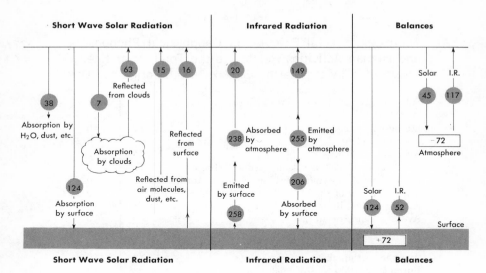

FIGURE 1–4 *Average annual radiation budget of the Earth. All units are in kilolangleys per year. Incoming solar radiation equals 263 kly yr⁻¹. Based on data from* W. D. Sellers, Physical Climatology, *University of Chicago Press, 1965.*

the Earth, must be radiated outward. Figure 1–4 shows how this is accomplished. The Earth emits 258 kly yr^{-1} of infrared radiation, of which 20 kly yr^{-1} escapes to outer space while 238 kly yr^{-1} are absorbed by atmospheric constituents, particularly by clouds, water vapor, and carbon dioxide. The same constituents in the atmosphere emit 355 kly yr^{-1} of which 206 are reabsorbed by the earth while 149 kly yr^{-1} escape to outer space. Thus, on the average there is a balance, as a total of 169 kly yr^{-1} of outgoing infrared radiation compensates for the same quantity of absorbed short wave solar radiation.

On the average over the Earth, the surface absorbs 124 kly yr^{-1} of solar radiation while it radiates 52 kly yr^{-1} of infrared radiation. The difference, 72 kly yr^{-1}, is called the *radiation balance* or *net radiation* of the Earth's surface. As noted in Fig. 1–4, the atmosphere absorbs only 45 kly yr^{-1} of solar radiation while radiating 117 kly yr.$^{-1}$ Therefore, the net radiation of the atmosphere is —72 kly yr.$^{-1}$

These results indicate that energy is transferred mostly from the Sun to the Earth's surface and then to the atmosphere. In order to prevent the Earth from getting too hot and the atmosphere from getting too cold, there must be a steady transport of heat from the Earth's surface (continents and oceans) to the atmosphere.

Heat Transport in Atmosphere and Oceans

In the preceding section, we considered the energy balance averaged over the Earth as a whole and found a positive net radiation at the surface which was balanced by a negative net radiation in the atmosphere. Such a balance does not exist at all latitudes. The net loss of radiation by the atmosphere is almost the same at all latitudes, but as shown in Fig. 1–5 the net gain of radiation by the surface is a maximum in tropical regions, decreases towards the poles and becomes negative around the poles.

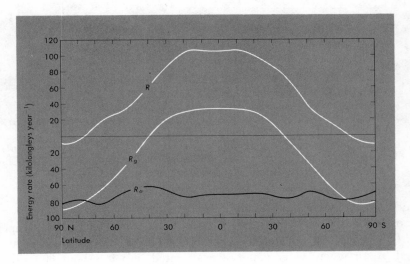

FIGURE 1–5   *The average annual latitudinal distribution of the radiation balances of the Earth's surface* R, *of the atmosphere* R_a, *and of the Earth-atmosphere system* R_g. *From W. D. Sellers,* Physical Climatology, University of Chicago Press, 1965.

The radiation balance of the earth-atmosphere system is positive equatorward of latitudes about 40° and negative at higher latitudes. If there were not a transfer of heat poleward in both hemispheres, the tropics would get progressively warmer. Since that has not happened, there must be a poleward transport of heat. The quantities of heat flow are shown in Fig. 1–6. In general, the maximum poleward heat flux occurs in the latitude band 40° to 50°.

It must be recognized that various forms of energy are transferred across

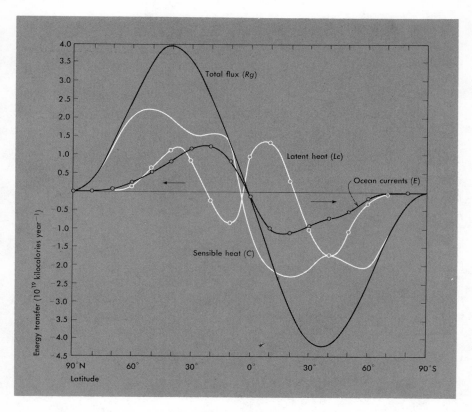

FIGURE 1–6 *The average annual latitudinal distribution of the components of the poleward energy flux in 10^{19} Kcal yr⁻¹. From W. D. Sellers,* Physical Climatology, *University of Chicago Press, 1965.*

latitude circles by air and ocean currents. *Sensible heat* is the energy represented by the motion of air molecules and is measured by the air temperature. It is carried by air and ocean currents. *Latent heat* is the energy absorbed by air when water vapor is evaporated into it. About 600 cal* of heat are absorbed when one gram of water evaporates. If a gram of water vapor condenses to form water drops, 600 cal of heat are released and can serve to warm up the air. In the atmosphere, substantial quantities of energy are transported in this way.

From an analysis of the curves in Fig. 1–6, it is found that the flux of latent heat accounts for 20 to 25 percent of the total energy transfer. The curves show that below about 22° latitude, water vapor and latent heat are carried equatorward, while at higher latitudes they are carried poleward.

The major poleward energy flux is by means of air motions. At low latitudes, on the average, there is a convectively driven longitudinal circula-

---

*The latent heat of vaporization of water depends on the temperature and varies from 569 to 629 cal g⁻¹ as the temperature varies from 50°C to −50°C.

tion. In such a circulation, the air rises near the equator, moves poleward at high altitudes, sinks at latitudes of about 30° and moves back towards the equator near the ground. Such a meridional circulation can account for the observed flux of heat. Details of the air currents will be examined in a later chapter.

In middle latitudes, the poleward transport of heat is by means of atmospheric disturbances causing cold air from high latitudes to move equatorward while warm air moves poleward. At latitudes of 50° and 70°, sensible heat flux accounts for most of the energy transfer.

In recent years, the role of the oceans in transporting heat has been more fully recognized. This is accomplished through the action of warm ocean currents traveling poleward while cold ocean currents move equatorward. The warm water moving under colder air gives off energy in the form of latent heat and sensible heat which directly warms the air. Figure 1–6 shows how ocean transport of energy varies with latitude, being most important in the lower latitudes. Overall, ocean currents may account for 20 to 25 percent of the total meridional heat transfer.

Vertical Structure of the Atmosphere

Since most of the incoming solar radiation which serves to heat up the air-earth-ocean system is absorbed at the surface, it seems reasonable to expect that, on the average, air temperatures are highest near the ground and decrease with altitude. That is precisely what happens in the lower atmosphere. At one time, it was thought that the temperature continued decreasing with altitude up to the top of the atmosphere. This idea was firmly put to rest with the invention of the radiosonde, a balloon-borne instrument which measures temperature, pressure and relative humidity. Subsequently, rocket-sounding techniques revealed the temperature structure of the atmosphere up to very high altitudes.

Before examining temperature variations, we must examine how atmospheric pressure changes with height and what is meant by the phrase "the top of the atmosphere." Its definition is somewhat arbitrary because of the gaseous nature of the atmosphere, but it can be defined in terms of atmospheric pressure.

Air pressure can be related to density (mass per unit volume) and temperature through the equation of state for an ideal gas. It is important to recognize that the pressure* is the weight of the air above a unit area. At

*Atmospheric pressure can be calculated from the ideal gas law is $P = RT/\rho$, where P is pressure, T is absolute temperature, ρ is density, R is the individual gas constant for air.

sea level, the average pressure of the Earth's atmosphere, in English units, can be expressed as about 14.7 lb in.$^{-2}$ This quantity is referred to as *one standard atmosphere*, and can be stated in a variety of units.

Meteorologists most often express atmospheric pressure in millibars (mb). This unit is a measurement of force per unit area in the metric system. One millbar equals 1,000 dynes cm^{-2}. Average sea level pressure is equal to 1,013.25 mb. For mathematical convenience, this number sometimes is rounded off and it is taken to be 1,000 mb.

Since the mass of air above a horizontal area decreases with height, the pressure also decreases with height in almost the same proportion. For most purposes one can disregard the small changes in gravity with height. Table 1–4 and Fig. 1–7 show that the 500-mb level which divides the atmospheric mass almost in half is at a mean altitude of about 5,600 m.

Table 1–4

Atmospheric Pressure as a Function of Altitude

Pressure	Percent of Sea Level Pressure	Altitude (km)
1,000. (approx.)	100.	0
500.	50.	5.6
100.	10.	16.2
10.	1.	31.2
1.	0.1	48.1
0.1	0.01	65.1
0.01	0.001	79.2
0.00003	0.00003	100.0

Table 1–4 also indicates that about 99.9 percent of the mass of the atmosphere is below about 50 km and 99.9997 percent is below 100 km. There still are gaseous constituents at higher altitudes but very few indeed. For the most part meteorologists focus on the properties and behavior of the lowest 30 km of the atmosphere. The quantities in Table 1–4 illustrate that in relation to the Earth's radius of about 6,400 km the atmosphere is a very shallow layer.

Figure 1.7 shows the average distribution of temperature with height. It is sometimes called the Standard Atmosphere. As expected, the temperature decreases with height up to an altitude of about 12 km where the trend changes abruptly. This level is called the *tropopause* and it separates the lower layer (the *troposphere*) from the next highest layer (the *stratosphere*).

The height of the tropopause varies with latitude; its mean altitude is about 18 km over the equator and 8 km over the poles. At any one place it

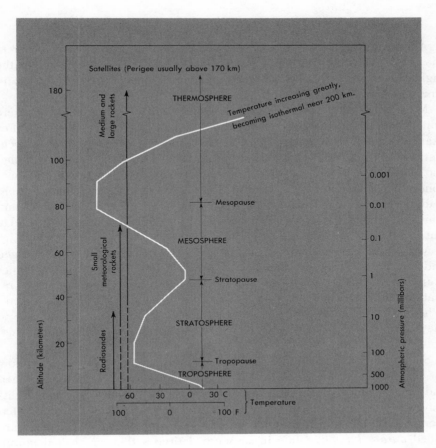

FIGURE 1–7   *Average temperature structure of the Earth's atmosphere and techniques used to probe various altitude ranges. From R. S. Quiroz,* Bulletin of American Meteorological Society, *1972,* **53***: 122–133.*

moves upward and downward with the passage of warm and cold air masses.

In the stratosphere the temperature gradually increases with height reaching a maximum at an altitude of about 50 km. This level is called the *stratopause*. The warm layer surrounding the stratopause can be attributed mostly to the absorption by ozone of solar ultraviolet radiation. Most atmospheric ozone is in the layer between 10 and 55 km. Although the peak concentrations are at about 30 km, small quantities of ozone near the top of the ozone layer effectively absorb most of the ultraviolet radiation.

In the *mesosphere* the temperature decreases with height up to about 80 km, the level known as the *mesopause*. Above it, there is a layer some 10 km thick with little temperature change. Still higher, through the thermosphere, the temperature increases with height.

General features of the Earth's atmosphere

Almost all the clouds and storm systems affecting life on earth occur in the troposphere. On the other hand, certain atmospheric processes in the higher layers of the atmosphere may influence low level pressure, wind and storm patterns in significant ways.

Many interesting geophysical phenomena occur in the upper atmosphere which are beyond the scope of topics we intend to cover in this book. For example, above about 80 km there is a deep region containing high concentrations of electrically charged particles and electrons. The layer is called the *ionosphere*. Before the advent of the communications satellite, the ionosphere played a unique and vital role in long range radio communications. Radio waves of particular kinds were "bounced" off the ionosphere and could be propagated over great distances. This technique is still used today but to a lesser extent than in the past.

Very short wave radiation from the Sun causes the ionization of nitrogen and oxygen atoms and molecules to produce the ionosphere. Sometimes eruptions on the surface of the Sun cause large increases of short wave radiation and increased ionization. The result is called a "magnetic storm." When gases below about 80 km become ionized, they cause an increase in the absorption of radio waves. As a result long distance radio communication is interrupted.

Solar eruptions also emit huge numbers of charged particles which follow the magnetic field of the earth. The high energy particles striking nitrogen and oxygen ionize them. The resulting emissions produce spectacular displays of lights in the form of arcs, rays, and curtains. They are most often seen over middle and high latitudes. In the Northern Hemisphere they are called *aurora borealis* while in southerly latitudes they are called *aurora australis*.

Nacreous clouds are members of a strikingly brilliant variety which occur at high altitudes (20 to 30 km) and have been mainly observed at northern latitudes in winter. They commonly are called mother-of-pearl clouds because of their beautiful pearly colorations when viewed during and just after, sunset. At still higher altitudes (75 to 90 km) at middle and high latitudes, *noctilucent* clouds are observed in rare instances. They can only be seen at twilight.

Readers interested in learning more about these fascinating, high-level phenomena are encouraged to pursue the topic in books on the upper atmosphere such as the ones by Richard Craig noted in the reading list.

2

Air motions and wind patterns

In order to explain weather and climate, it is necessary to have an understanding of the patterns of air motion and the factors controlling them.

The atmosphere is a restless medium; it almost never stops moving. Sometimes the air speeds are so low that flags hang limply from their staffs and anemometer cups on the roof of a weather station do not turn at all. But even on such occasions a very sensitive measuring system would usually find some air movement. At the other end of the wind velocity spectrum one finds tornadoes and hurricanes in which the winds may reach perhaps 100 m sec^{-1} (224 mph).

Although air motions are three dimensional, it is convenient to examine the horizontal motion and the vertical motion separately. When meteorologists use the term "wind," they are referring to the horizontal components of velocity. The upwards and downwards motions are often called updrafts and downdrafts, particularly when considering conditions in clouds having strong vertical velocities.

Vertical Air Motions

Vertical motions in the atmosphere can be produced in a number of ways. Some are obvious. For example, air rises when it is forced to move over rising terrain. When the direction of flow is over a gradually sloping region such as the Western Great Plains, the upward velocities are fairly small, perhaps 10 cm sec^{-1}. On the other hand, if air is blown against a steep mountain barrier its vertical velocities can amount to several meters per second.

Air is also lifted over weather fronts. As will be seen in the next chapter, when large bodies of cold and warm air come into contact they do not mix readily. Instead the cold, heavier air sinks in wedge-like fashion under the warmer, less dense air. The transition between the warm and cold air is called a *front*. As the cold air advances, the warm air it displaces is caused to rise.

Meteorologists sometimes refer to the initial vertical velocity of the air produced by the terrain or by frontal surfaces as being "mechanically" induced. A crucial consideration is whether the air accelerates or decelerates after it has started to move vertically. The answers are supplied by an examination of Newton's second law of motion which equates net force to acceleration. It can be shown that the most important force is a buoyancy force. In the simplest terms, when a volume of air is warmer than the surroundings it rises; when it is colder it sinks. To be more exact, it is necessary to consider the air density rather than merely the temperature. Water vapor reduces the density of air because the molecular weight of water vapor is 18 while that of air is 28.9. As a result, the more humid the air, the less its density and the greater the buoyancy force. In general, humidity differences have smaller effect than temperature differences in determining the buoyancy of a volume of air.

When analyzing the buoyancy of air containing cloud droplets, ice crystals, and raindrops, it is necessary to determine how their masses affect the overall density of a unit volume of air. Liquid or ice particles increase the overall density of the volume of air in which they exist because the densities of water and ice are about 1 g cm^{-3} while the density of air ranges from about 1.2 x 10^{-3} g cm^{-3} at sea level to 0.3 x 10^{-3} at 12 km. The total masses of liquid or ice particles are small in relation to the mass of air in the same volume. For example, at an altitude of about 2 km, a cubic meter of air has a mass of about 10^3 g while the mass of water in liquid and frozen form in a typical cloud is almost always less than 10 g. Nevertheless, the relatively small mass of water may have significant effects on the buoyancy forces particularly at higher altitudes.

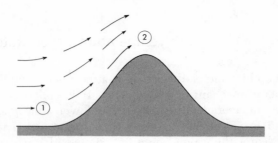

FIGURE 2–1 *Air moving over a hill is forced to rise from altitude 1 to altitude 2.*

Imagine a volume of air beginning to rise as it passes over a hill. If, after ascending to a certain level as shown in Fig. 2.1, the air is less dense than the air in the surroundings, it will be subjected to an upwards buoyancy force. As a result, there will be an upward acceleration of the already rising air.

In the case just described, the atmosphere is said to be *unstable*. This state exists when a volume of air, displaced from one level to another and then released, continues to accelerate in the direction of the displacement. When the air is unstable, vertical motions both up and down are accelerated by buoyancy forces.

Under certain atmospheric conditions, when a volume of air is lifted to a higher altitude, it arrives there colder and more dense than the surrounding air. In this case, there is a downward buoyancy force and, the volume of displaced air is forced back towards the level of origin. In such circumstances, the atmosphere is *stable*.

If a lifted volume of air arrives at a new altitude having the same temperature and density as the surrounding air, there will be no net buoyancy force. The volume will remain at the new level and the atmosphere is said to have *neutral stability*.

The importance of atmospheric stability will become more evident as the discussion progresses. On days when the atmosphere is unstable, rising volumes of air are accelerated rapidly upwards. Low flying airplanes experience turbulence caused by strong ascending and descending columns of air. If the air is humid, bulging cumulus clouds may form and result in thunderstorms.

When the air is stable, vertical air motions are suppressed. When such a stable layer occurs in the lowest hundred meters of the atmosphere, there is little mixing of air near the Earth's surface with cleaner air aloft. If there are prolific sources of air pollutants such as smoke stacks and motor vehicles, the absence of vertical mixing can lead to dangerous increases in the concentration of pollutants in the air. Well-known air-pollution disasters, such as the ones in London in 1952 and in Donora, Pennsylvania in 1948, occurred when stable air covered these areas for several days.

Temperature Lapse Rate

The chief factor determining atmospheric stability is the rate at which temperature changes with height. It is called the *lapse rate*. Figure 1–7 shows the average lapse rate in the lower atmosphere to be 0.65°C per 100 m (3.5°F per 1000 ft.). At any time and at any place, it can be very different. Nearer the ground on a hot summer day it would be much greater. At night, particularly on a clear, cloudless night, the temperature often increases with height. The layer through which this occurs, is known as a *temperature inversion* (see Fig. 2–2).

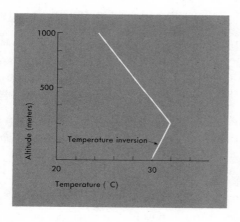

FIGURE 2–2 *At night, when sky is clear and air is dry, a temperature inversion frequently forms near the ground.*

Temperature inversions exert important influences on many atmospheric processes. As will be seen in the paragraphs to follow, they are layers of marked vertical stability, and therefore they act to suppress vertical motions.

There are various explanations for the formation of temperature inversions. The ones in the lowest layers of the atmosphere often occur as a result of cooling of the Earth's surface by radiation. In clear, dry places, the Earth begins to cool in the late afternoon when the outgoing infrared radiation is greater than the incoming, short wave, solar radiation. After sunset, radiative heat loss proceeds rapidly. As the ground cools, heat from the lowest layers of the air is transported to the ground and radiated outward. This leads to a cooling of a shallow layer of air near the ground and the formation of a temperature inversion.

In a desert locality such as Tucson, Arizona, ground-level temperature inversions are common in the early morning hours and rare during the warm part of the day (see Table 2–1). The table shows that in the winter, when

Air motions and wind patterns

Table 2-1

Percent Frequency of Temperature Inversions
Below 150 m at Tucson, Arizona

	Time—MST			
	0500	0800	1700	2000
Winter	89	83	21	65
Summer	74	15	4	19

Source: Hosler, C. R., Low-Level Inversion Frequency
in the Contiguous United States. *Mon. Wea. Rev.*, 1961.
Vol. 89, pp. 319–339.

the Sun rises later and sets earlier, the temperature inversions persist later in the mornings and start to form earlier in the evening.

In some cases, low-level temperature inversions continue for days. Usually this occurs when warm air passes over a cold surface. For example, inversions form just above the ground when tropical air from the Gulf of Mexico moves northward over the United States during the winter. Also, temperature inversions frequently are produced when warm air moves over colder water. When this happens, the air loses heat to the underlying surface by means of conduction and small scale turbulent diffusion. The end result is a persistent, low-level temperature inversion.

Various types of temperature inversions are consistently observed in the atmosphere. At high levels we encounter the stratosphere which is defined as the layer where the temperature remains nearly constant or increases with height (Fig. 1–7). Because of its marked stability, the stratosphere places a lid on the growth of giant thunderstorms. Powerful updrafts sometimes penetrate the tropopause with vertical velocities which might exceed 50 m sec^{-1}, but they are rapidly decelerated by the negative buoyancy forces of the stable air in the stratosphere.

Since thunderstorms and other precipitating systems do not extend significantly into the stratosphere and the stability suppresses mixing between troposphere and stratosphere, pollutants introduced into the latter by volcanic eruptions, nuclear explosions or aircraft remain for a long time. Table 2–2 shows the estimated residence times of particulate pollutants in various layers of the atmosphere.

Following the eruptions of powerful volcanoes such as Krakatoa in 1883 and Agung in 1963, massive quantities of dust particles were injected into the stratosphere. They increased the overall turbidity of the atmosphere as shown in Fig. 1–2 and were removed from the atmosphere very slowly.

Temperature inversions are common throughout the troposphere. As you

Air motions and wind patterns

Table 2–2

Residence Times of Particulate Pollutants in the Atmosphere

Layer	Residence Times
Lower troposphere	1–3 weeks
Upper troposphere	2–4 weeks
Lower stratosphere	6–12 months
Upper stratosphere	3–5 years

Source: *Man's Impact on the Global Environment*, Report at the Study of Critical Environmental Problems (SCEP). M.I.T. Press, 1970.

would expect, the frontal zone separating cold air under a front from warmer air above it, generally is an isothermal or an inversion layer. The stability of the zone acts to reduce the mixture of cold and warm air and serves to maintain the front as a weather system develops and moves.

Many inversions in the lower atmosphere are attributable to sinking air. As a volume of air subsides, it moves to lower altitudes where the pressure is higher. The higher pressure causes the air to be compressed and this process increases the temperature of the sinking air. More will be said about this process in the next section. In some instances the subsidence continues to a particular level and then the air diverges horizontally. A temperature inversion is commonly observed in the layer separating the upper region of sinking air and the lower region where there is almost no net vertical motions.

Subsidence inversions are frequently found in regions of high pressure because, as will be seen later, they are characterized by sinking air. The subsidence also acts to inhibit cloud formation. As a result during the night in high pressure regions, you often observe a radiation inversion at the ground and at the same time, a subsidence inversion aloft (Fig. 2–3).

Over the vast areas of the low latitude semipermanent high pressure zones, temperature inversions are a normal part of the atmospheric structure. Over the oceans in particular, they separate a moist layer of air near the ground from a dry layer above the inversion.

The high pressure region dominating the eastern North Pacific extends over southern California and explains the prevailing sunny skies. It also accounts for a persistent subsidence inversion at an altitude of about 700 m. Under the inversion, pollutants from motor vehicles and industry become concentrated and lead to the famous Los Angeles smog.

Air motions and wind patterns

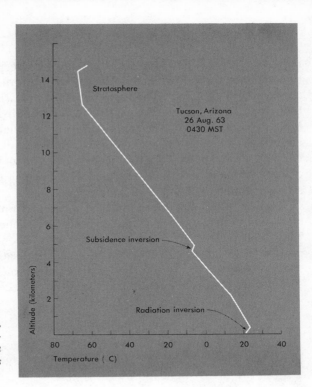

FIGURE 2–3 *Occasionally, at night, a subsidence inversion occurs aloft and a radiation inversion occurs near the ground.*

Adiabatic Lapse Rate

The reason why stability depends on the temperature lapse rate can be seen by examining what happens when a volume of air rises or sinks in the atmosphere. Consider a small volume of air which we will call a "parcel" of air. As it ascends from altitude 1 to altitude 2 in Fig. 2–4, it moves to a region of lower pressure. In the process, the volume of the parcel expands until the pressure inside equals the pressure outside it. The expansion

FIGURE 2–4 *Rising dry air cools at the adiabatic rate of 1°C per 100 meters of altitude change.*

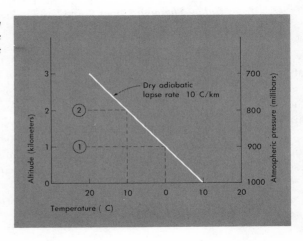

requires that work be done and the energy to do it is supplied by heat extracted from the parcel of air. Energy in the form of heat is converted to another form of energy. The temperature of the rising parcel decreases even though no heat is carried away from the expanding air. This is called *adiabatic* cooling. In the Earth's atmosphere, the adiabatic cooling rate of dry air is 1°C for each 100 m of ascent. A descending volume of dry air is warmed at a rate of 1°C/100 m. As it moves to higher pressure, there is compression and work is converted to heat which causes an increase in the air temperature.

Knowing the adiabatic lapse rate and the temperature lapse rate in the atmosphere, it is easy to establish if the atmosphere is stable or unstable. This point is illustrated in Fig. 2–5. It can be seen, that when the environmental lapse rate is greater than the adiabatic rate, the atmosphere is unstable because a rising parcel will become warmer than the environment. The positive buoyancy force causes the air to accelerate upwards.

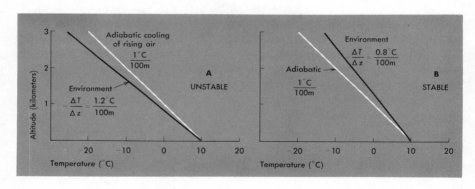

FIGURE 2–5 *When the environmental temperature lapse rate $\Delta T/\Delta z$ exceeds 1°C/100 m (the adiabatic rate), the rising air remains warmer than the environment and is unstable. When $\Delta T/\Delta z$ is less than 1°C/100 m, the atmosphere is stable. The figure gives examples of values of $\Delta T/\Delta z$.*

When the environmental lapse rate is less than the adiabatic rate the atmosphere is stable. This is particularly the case when a temperature inversion exists. If the environmental lapse rate is exactly 1°C/100 m, the atmosphere will be in neutral equilibrium. A rising or descending parcel of air will always have the same temperature as the surroundings.

In this discussion we have considered only convective motions when the air is "dry." This does not mean that the air contains no water vapor but rather that there has been no condensation or evaporation.

Air motions and wind patterns

Vertical Motions of Moist Air

As already noted, rising air expands and cools. As it does so, the relative humidity of the air increases. This quantity can be defined in various ways. For example it can be written as the fraction, expressed in percent, of the mass of water vapor in the air divided by the maximum mass the air can hold at the same temperature. Another definition of the relative humidity is that it is the fraction, expressed in percent, of the actual vapor pressure of the air divided by the saturation vapor pressure at the same temperature. As the air temperature decreases, the denominator of the fraction decreases, (Fig. 2–6) and the relative humidity increases.

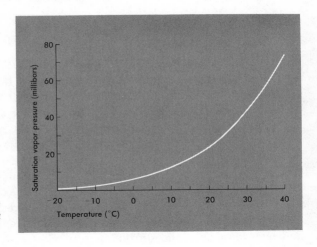

FIGURE 2–6 *The saturation vapor pressure as a function of temperature.*

If rising air is sufficiently humid, an ascent of only a few hundred meters could cause the relative humidity to reach 100 percent. At times when the air is dry, it might have to rise many kilometers before it becomes saturated. When it does so, condensation begins, and a cloud starts to form. In the process, the latent heat of vaporization is released into the air and warms it. As noted in Chapter 1, it amounts to about 600 calories for each gram of water condensed.

Before condensation begins, the rising air parcel cools at the dry adiabatic rate (Fig. 2–7). After condensation and cloud formation start, the added latent heat partially offsets the cooling caused by expansion. As a result, further ascent leads to slower cooling than the 1°C/100 m repre-

Air motions and wind patterns

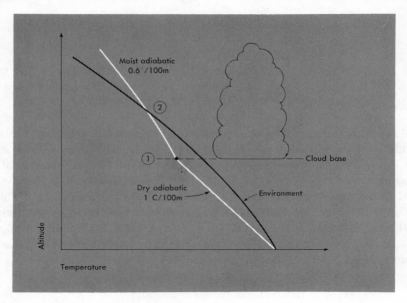

FIGURE 2-7 *Changes in temperature of a rising volume of humid air.*

senting the dry adiabatic rate. When condensation is occurring, a rising volume of air cools at the *moist adiabatic rate*. It varies with temperature and pressure, but in the lower part of the atmosphere is about 0.6°C/100 m.

In the example in Fig. 2-7, the air is stable for dry air. If a volume of air is forced to ascend from the ground to point 1, it becomes progressively cooler and more dense with respect to the surrounding air. At level 1, condensation begins and the rising air cools at the moist adiabatic rate. Between levels 1 and 2 the ascending air continues to have a downward buoyancy force exerted on it, and it still is necessary for a "mechanical force" to be applied in order for it to rise. Above level 2, however, the ascending parcel of air finds itself in an unstable environment; it is warmer and less dense than the surrounding air. The resulting upwards buoyancy force causes an upwards acceleration of the cloud air. Continued convection could result in the formation of towering convective clouds and possibly the growth of thunderstorms containing strong updrafts and downdrafts. More will be said on this subject in a later chapter.

Horizontal Air Motions—The Winds

Air can be treated as a fluid and its motions studied in the manner used to study the motion of other fluids—the ocean waters, for example. In order to do this it is necessary to know the forces exerted on any volume of air. The net force, F, can be equated to the product of mass, m, and acceleration, *a*, of the air as specified by Newton's second law of motion, $F = ma$.

If the Earth were flat and stationary, the motion of the air would be specified in terms of pressure forces and frictional forces. Let us consider them separately.

As noted earlier, atmospheric pressure is the weight of air over a unit area in a column extending to the top of the atmosphere. The weight depends on the density of the air in the column, and the density in turn, depends on the air temperature and to a lesser extent on the humidity of the air. As the air density through a column of air varies, the pressure at its base does also. If the pressure at the ground and the height distributions of temperature and moisture are known, the pressure at any altitude can be calculated, to a good degree of approximation by means of the *hydrostatic equation.** This states that the pressure difference between any altitude z_1, and a higher altitude z_2 is the weight of the air, in a column of unit cross-sectional area, between z_2 and z_1. By taking a series of altitude layers the pressure at succeedingly higher altitudes can be calculated.

Atmospheric pressure at any altitude varies in time and space. Every weather map shows regions of low pressure and regions of high pressure. In order to account for these regions, it is necessary to examine the entire column of air above the area. For example, low pressure regions do occur with cold air near the ground. If the entire atmosphere were examined, however, it would be found that on the average the air density over the area of low pressure would be less than the air density in surrounding regions.

When the pressure differs from one point to another, there is a pressure force exerted on the air (Fig. 2–8). It is directed from high to low pressure and is proportional to a quantity called the *pressure gradient* which measures the rate of change of pressure with distance. On a weather map the pattern of pressure may be represented by *isobars*, that is, lines along which the pressure is the same. When the pressure difference between points p_2 and p_1 measured along a line perpendicular to the isobars is divided by the distance between p_2 and p_1, the pressure gradient is obtained. The closer the isobars, the greater the pressure-gradient force.

---

*The hydrostatic equation is $p_1 - p_2 = Dg \, (z_2 - z_1)$ where D is the average density; g is the acceleration of gravity; p_2 and p_1 are the pressures at altitude z_2 and z_1, respectively. For example, if p_1, the pressure at sea level is 1013 mb, and the average density, D, between the surface ($z = 0$) and $z = 1$ km is 1.1×10^{-3} g cm^{-3},

$$p_1 - p_2 = 1.1 \times 10^{-3} \, \frac{g}{cm^3} \times 980 \, \frac{cm}{sec^2} \times 10^5 \, cm$$

$$= 108 \times 10^3 \, \left(\frac{g \; cm}{sec^2} \right) \frac{1}{cm^2} = 108 \times 10^3 \, \frac{dynes}{cm^2} = 108 \, mb$$

Therefore, p_2, the pressure at an altitude of 1 km $= (1013 - 108) = 905$ mb.

Air motions and wind patterns

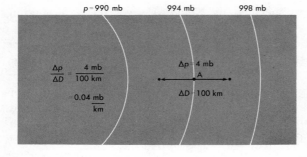

Fig. 2–8 *The pressure force increases as the pressure gradient increases. In this example, the pressure gradient at point A is 0.04 mb km⁻¹.*

Frictional forces in the atmosphere come into play when the air begins to move. They include frictional effects of the ground as well as stresses between slow and fast moving air. Friction forces act in a direction opposite to the direction of motion and serve to reduce the wind speed.

On a hypothetical stationary, flat surface, the sum of the pressure and frictional forces could be equated to the acceleration of the air and used to obtain fields of motion. In fact, because the Earth is nearly spherical and rotating once every 24 hours, the task of specifying motions in the atmosphere becomes complicated.

The chief difficulty arises because of the way we sense and measure air motions. Air motions are represented in terms of a coordinate system fixed on a rotating, spherical Earth. This is done for the obvious reason that we reside on this planet.

The effects of the Earth's rotation are usually taken into account by meteorologists by the introduction of a concept called the "Coriolis force." Contrary to the impression given in many books, it is a complicated concept and difficult to explain briefly and simply. Some notion of what is involved can be illustrated in the common example of the case of a missile fired southward from the North Pole (Fig. 2–9). An observer in space sees it moving along a straight line. On the other hand, during its southward pas-

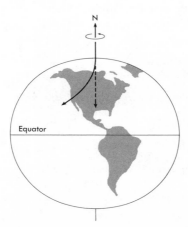

Figure 2–9 *To an observer on the Earth, a missile fired towards the south from the North Pole appears to curve towards the right, as shown by the solid line. From outer space the missile would be seen following the dashed line as the Earth rotated beneath it.*

sage, the earth rotates from west to east under the trajectory. The missile strikes the ground at a point which is to the west of the point directly along the direction towards which it was launched. To a person on the Earth, it would appear that the missile followed the trajectory curving towards the west. It would appear that there was a force acting on the missile and deflecting it towards the right.

If a parcel of air at the North Pole were forced to move southward under the effects of a pressure gradient, it would also be subjected to a deflection to the right as was the missile. In writing the equations of motion of air, this effect of the Earth's rotation is taken into account by including a Coriolis force term. The apparent force causing a deflection towards the right can be shown to act regardless of the direction of the air motion, but it varies with the sine of the latitude, being a maximum at the poles and zero at the equator. In the Southern Hemisphere, the Coriolis force acts to the left of the direction of the wind velocity.

The net effect of the real pressure and friction forces and the apparent Coriolis force, are illustrated in Fig. 2–10. In the Northern Hemisphere, at

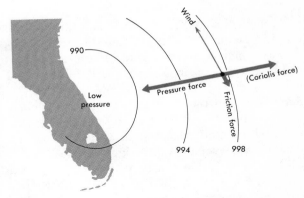

FIGURE 2–10 *A volume of air is acted on by the real forces caused by pressure differences and friction and by the apparent Coriolis force. The excess of the pressure force over the Coriolis force accounts for winds nearly parallel to the isobars but having a small deviation towards the center of low pressure.*

altitudes above about one kilometer where frictional effects are small, the winds tend to blow nearly parallel to the isobars with low pressure on the left when looking downward. This is known as the Buys Ballot Law. In the Southern Hemisphere the relation is reversed. If one assumes that frictional forces equal zero and the pressure force is exactly balanced by the Coriolis force, the wind is called *geostrophic* and it is parallel to the isobars.

Frictional effects, which are greatest near the Earth's surface, act to slow down the wind and produce a deflection of the winds across the isobars towards lower pressure. As a result, near the ground, air converges towards a center of low pressure and away from a center of high pressure.

Air motions and wind patterns

Local Circulations

The relations discussed in the preceding section can explain many of the wind patterns seen on daily weather maps, particularly on the maps of the upper atmosphere. They are based on observations of such quantities as pressure, temperature and wind at stations several hundred miles apart.

There are many types of wind circulations of a local nature which are difficult to explain on the basis of the standard observation. They occur because of peculiarities of topography whose effects are often missed by the widely spaced weather stations. Several examples can be given.

Along coast lines, it is common to experience sea breezes on summer afternoons (Fig. 2–11). They occur because the Sun's rays increase the temperature of the land and the air just above it more than they raise the temperature of the air over the water. As a result, a low-altitude pressure gradient develops from water to land. Cool air from over the sea (or lake) moves over the land and bathes the coast with sea breezes. Over the land, air rises, moves out to sea aloft, and sinks over the sea in a form of a convection cell.

At night the land cools faster than the water and the sea-breeze circulation is sometimes reversed. When this occurs, a light wind from land to sea develops and is called a land breeze.

In mountainous areas, particularly in desert regions, it is common to find what are known as mountain and valley winds. During the daytime the Sun's rays heat the air over the mountain slopes. As the air warms, it becomes buoyant and flows upslope, that is up the valley. At night, heat is radiated to outer space, the air cools, becomes more dense and a mountain wind flows downhill. When skies are clear and the air is dry, heating and cooling by radiation can be very effective in causing mountain and valley breezes. For example, in Tucson, Arizona where these conditions often prevail, the afternoon wind blows upslope, that is from the northwest on more than 50 percent of the days. During the early morning hours, the wind blows from the southeast (downslope) on about 80 percent of the days.

It is evident that the nature of many local circulations are largely determined by interactions of atmosphere and the underlying Earth. The low-

FIGURE 2–11 *Sea breeze and land breeze circulations.*

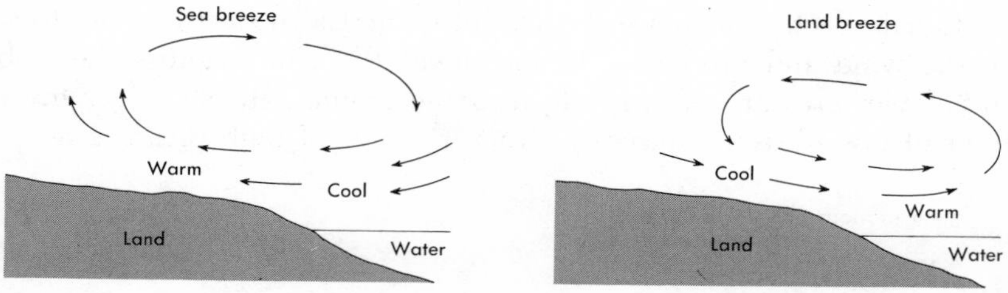

level air temperature depends on whether the surface is land or water; furthermore, it is influenced in an important way by the characteristics of the land and the water. For example, the temperature over a light, wet sand would be lower than over a dark, dry barren field. The sand would reflect sunlight more effectively than the dark soil. Furthermore, part of the insolation would be used to evaporate water leaving less heat to increase the temperature.

Some unusual circulations of a local character can not be explained entirely by a consideration of the local characteristics of Earth and atmosphere. They result from the interaction of local effects with certain large scale features of the atmosphere. For example, the warm, dry winds called *foehns* in Europe occur in such a fashion. They are frequently observed on the northern slopes of the Alps, but they also are common on the east slopes of the Rocky Mountains, particularly in Wyoming and Montana where they usually are called *chinooks*. They may occur over any mountain range if the appropriate conditions occur.

Foehn winds are initiated by the advance of an upper level, low-pressure center. A low pressure trough is formed on the lee side of the mountain range. When the low-pressure center aloft passes over the mountain ridge, strong downslope winds develop on the lee side of the mountain. The sinking air driven downward by the low-level pressure gradient forces is warmed by adiabatic compression. This also causes a reduction in the relative humidity. As a result, the foehn winds are hot and dry.

Since the foehn air replaces much colder air, there can be sudden, intense warming. It has been reported that on one occasion, at Havre, Montana, a chinook caused the temperature to increase from 11° to 42°F (−11.7° to 5.6°C) in 3 minutes. Increases of air temperature of 10° to 20°C in 15 minutes are not unusual.

The high temperature coupled with low humidity can lead to rapid melting and evaporation of snow. It has been reported that 30 cm of snow can disappear in a few hours in a strong chinook.

There are many other examples of wind circulations which come into being as a result of interaction of atmospheric systems with the land and sea. A well known, large-scale example which is of crucial importance in the lives of nations is the *monsoon*. In India alone, changes in the character of the summer monsoon and its rainfall can mean the difference between life and death for millions of people. Some of its features are reviewed in the next chapter.

3

Planetary patterns of air motion

The atmosphere is sometimes called a heat engine because it is a system which receives energy in the form of heat, converts some of it to kinetic energy, and does work. Only a small fraction of the incoming solar radiation is transformed into the kinetic energy of air motions. Of the roughly 10^{14} kw of power received from the Sun, about 2×10^{12} kw are converted into kinetic energy. The atmospheric engine therefore has an efficiency of only about two percent. This makes it a very inefficient engine, but nevertheless the available supply of kinetic energy in the winds is still enough to dwarf all man-made power sources.

When observing the fields of air motion in the Earth's atmosphere, it is important to recognize that there are many scales of motion. For example, on the lowest scale, there are gusts of wind having a dimension of centimeters and a duration of seconds. Swirling dust devils over the desert have diameters of meters and lifetimes of minutes. Squall winds under thunderstorms cover areas which can be kilometers across and may last for hours. The cyclones and anticyclones to be discussed later have dimensions from hundreds to thousands of kilometers and last for days.

At the largest scale of atmospheric motion are the planetary wave patterns extending over a major fraction of the entire planet. They are part of the *general circulation* of the atmosphere.

In order to understand patterns of weather and climate, it is necessary to appreciate the characteristics of the general circulation, the factors controlling it, and its interaction with smaller scale circulations.

Description of the General Circulation

If you examine a series of weather maps depicting pressure and wind patterns over the Earth, you find them changing continuously as pressures rise in some regions and fall in others. Centers of low and high pressure may weaken and strengthen markedly over half a day. Over a period of a few days, centers of low or high pressure disappear and new ones form. A casual examination might give the impression of a random series of unrelated events in time and position. Such an idea, however, is not in accordance with the behavior of the atmosphere. Certain important features of the general circulation, because of their persistent nature, show up clearly if weather maps for many years are averaged.

An idealized version of the wind patterns over the Earth is shown in Fig. 3–1. As a result of the pressure forces associated with the belt of high pressure at about 30°N, there are persistent northeast *trade winds* at low latitudes. In middle latitudes there are prevailing westerly winds and another belt of easteries at still higher latitudes. In the Southern Hemisphere a somewhat similar pattern prevails.

On the average, in regions of low pressure, air tends to rise and be accompanied by clouds and precipitation. It is not surprising to find that in equatorial regions, where the trade winds converge, the air generally ascends. Since it is often quite humid, the result is heavy rainfall. The regions where the trades meet is called the *intertropical convergence zone* (ITC) or the *equatorial low pressure trough*. It is an area where surface winds are generally light and for this reason it was named the *doldrums* many years ago. On the average the air ascends over the ITC, moves poleward and descends in the regions of higher pressure in the subtropics. This circulation resembles a giant convection cell.

The sinking air in the high pressure areas inhibits cloud formation. Persistence of such conditions leads to the excessively dry weather which is associated with deserts. An examination of climatological charts (see Chap-

FIGURE 3–1 *Simplified schematic drawing of the general circulation of the atmosphere.*

ter 7) reveals that the deserts of the world are mostly under the regions of high pressure located along the bands centered at about 30 degrees latitude in both hemispheres. Near the center of the high pressure areas, the winds are light. In the days of the sailing ships, vessels were sometimes becalmed for long periods. This region was named the *horse latitudes*, presumably because horses had to be dropped over the side when the supply of food and water ran out.

The picture of the general circulation represented in Fig. 3–1 is a highly simplified one, but it does serve to identify some of the principal features of the overall pressure and wind patterns. More realistic pictures of part of the general circulation are given by Fig. 3–2A and Fig. 3–2B. They show average sea-level pressure and the wind patterns during January and July. Some of the similarities with the schematic diagram pictured in Fig. 3–1 are obvious. The charts also indicate some important characteristics which are not evident in the simplified schematic. The bands of high and low pressure are not continuous around the Earth. Instead, there are distinct and pronounced centers in geographically favored positions.

Planetary patterns of air motion

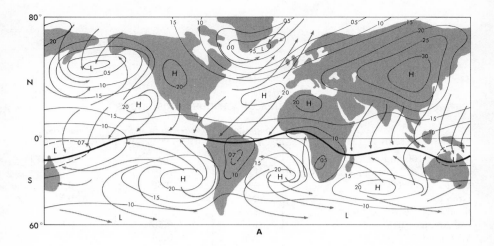

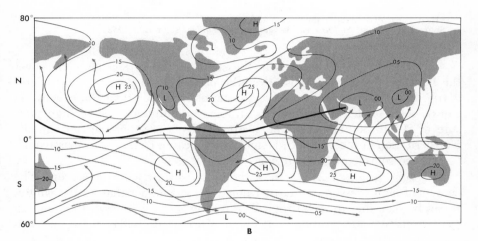

FIGURE 3–2 *Average sea-level winds and pressures (isobars in millibars exceeding 1,000 mb) over the earth in (A) January and (B) July. The heavy solid line is the intertropical convergence zone. From* Introduction to the Atmosphere *by Herbert Riehl. Copyright 1965. Used with permission of McGraw-Hill Book Company.*

In the summer hemisphere, the land areas are warmer than the ocean areas. (See the maps in Fig. 7–2). The Sun's heat is absorbed and distributed over a relatively shallow layer of soil and rocks. Furthermore, the specific heats and heat capacities of these substances is smaller than that of water (Table 3–1). This means that a given quantity of heat will raise the temperature of a unit mass of land more than the temperature of the same quantity of water. More important, the incoming solar radiation penetrates into the water to a depth of many meters and because of the vertical and horizontal mixing, the heat is distributed through a large mass of water.

Planetary patterns of air motion

Table 3–1

Thermal Properties of Various Substances

Substance	Density (g cm^{-3})	Specific Heat (cal gm^{-1} °C^{-1})	Heat Capacity* (cal cm^{-3} °C^{-1})
Air ($p = 1000$ mb; $T = 0$°C)	0.0013	0.24	0.00031
Quartz sand (medium fine, dry)	1.65	0.19	0.31
Ice ($T = 0$°C)	0.92	0.50	0.46
Granite	2.7	0.19	0.51
Sandy clay (15% water)	1.78	0.33	0.59
Calcareous earth (43% water)	1.67	0.53	0.88
Wet mud	1.50	0.60	0.90
Water	1.0	1.0	1.0

*Heat capacity is density times specific heat.
Source: R. J. List, *Smithsonian Meteorological Tables*, Sixth Ed., 1958.

Over the warmer continents in the summer, the surface pressures over the land are lower than those over the oceans. In the winter the reverse is true because the continents are substantially colder than the oceans. As can be seen, in the winter there is an almost continuous belt of high pressure at 20° to 30° latitude. The seasonal effects are more obvious in the Northern than in the Southern Hemisphere because of the more massive nature of the continents in the former.

The maps in Fig. 3–2 show how the patterns shift with the seasons. The centers of high pressure are farther north in the summer than in the winter. It can be seen that the intertropical convergence zone "follows the Sun." In January its average position is at about 5°S latitude while in July it averages about 10°N latitude.

Two striking features of the January map are the pronounced low pressure centers over the Aleutian Islands and Iceland. In winter they are persistent and have an important influence on Northern Hemisphere weather.

Another feature of these maps which deserves notice is the *monsoon* winds over the Asian subcontinent. In winter the flow is from the cold continent toward the Indian Ocean; in summer it reverses direction. There is a broad current from over the ocean towards the low pressure areas of southern Asia. As the humid, unstable air passes over land, and particularly when it encounters the Himalaya Mountains, it ascends producing torrential showers and thunderstorms. Some places such as Cherrapunji, India average an almost incredible 11 meters of rainfall per year, most of it during the summer monsoon.

The patterns of pressure and wind are smoother in the upper atmosphere than at the surface. Figure 3–3 shows average conditions at the 500-mb

Planetary patterns of air motion

level (altitude about 5,600 meters above sea level). This is a particularly significant level because it divides the atmosphere almost in half, i.e., about half the total mass is above the 500-mb level while the other half is below it. Note that in Fig. 3–3, we have introduced the idea of depicting properties of the atmosphere on a surface of *constant pressure*. In earlier discussions we examined the variation of pressure on a horizontal surface and observed if the pressure was high or low. When considering a surface over which the pressure is constant it is possible to measure how the height above sea level varies from place to place and time to time. A region which appears as one of high pressure on a constant height surface appears as a region of high altitude on a constant pressure surface.

FIGURE 3–3   *Average 500-mb charts over the Northern Hemisphere in (A) January, and (B, next page) July. The heavy lines show the height of the 500-mb level in tens of feet. From Technical Report 21, U.S. Department of Commerce, NOAA, 1952.*

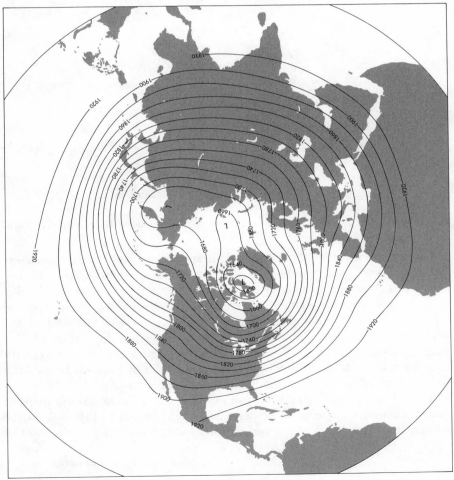

A

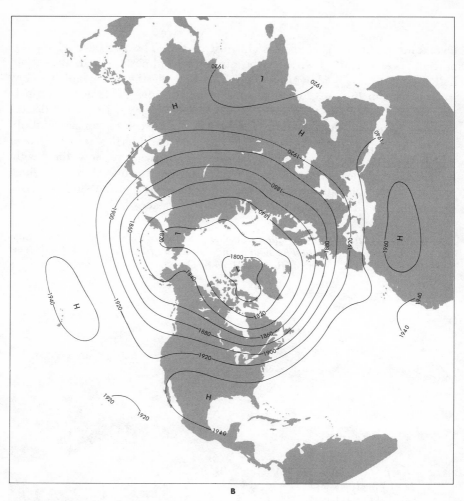

FIGURE 3–3 (B) Average 500-mb charts over the Northern Hemisphere in July.

Because of various advantages in interpretation, particularly when examining maps at a number of altitudes, meteorologists generally use constant-pressure maps rather than constant-height maps. It sometimes disturbs people accustomed to using constant-altitude charts, but if you are interested primarily in the patterns of high and low pressure and of the winds there should be no confusion. Lows and highs in the surface of constant pressure coincide with lows and highs of pressure, respectively. In addition the winds tend to blow parallel to the lines of constant height, and the wind speed increases as the height gradient increases.

With these points in mind, we can examine the average 500-mb maps of the Northern Hemisphere in January and July depicted in Fig. 3–3. In the winter, there are two low pressure centers located generally to the west of

Planetary patterns of air motion

their surface counterparts over the Aleutians and Iceland. Except for these distinct centers, you see a broad current of winterly winds at most latitudes which blow through long wave patterns. Over the United States, western Europe, and the western Pacific, the lines of constant height dip towards the south. They are called long-wave troughs and are separated by long-wave ridges.

In summer the average 500-mb map is substantially different than in winter. The high latitude lows disappear, the westerlies are weaker, and there is a belt of high pressure areas at low latitudes. To the south of this belt there are easterly winds at the 500-mb level. Some easterlies are also found in the winter but they are usually nearer the equator.

One of the striking features of the circulation pattern in the Earth's atmosphere becomes dramatically evident when a vertical cross section from north to south is examined (Fig. 3–4). There is a strong current of air having a pronounced maximum, which on the average, in the Northern Hemisphere exceeds 60 m sec^{-1}. This current is called the *jet stream*. Its center is located at an altitude of about 12 km and it extends around the globe, sometimes with no interruption. Its path meanders northward and southward, and as a result, average constant altitude charts tend to smooth out the wind pattern.

FIGURE 3–4   *A schematic vertical cross section extending north–south in the Northern Hemisphere through the polar front (heavy lines) and showing the wind profile through a jet stream. The speeds are in meters per second and temperatures in °C. From E. Palmén and C. W. Newton,* Atmospheric Circulation Systems, *Academic Press, 1969.*

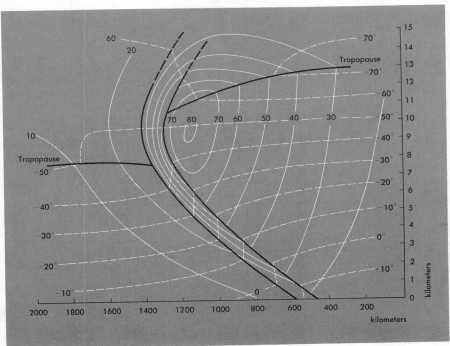

The jet stream plays a crucial role in governing the behavior of the atmosphere. It is a means for the rapid propagation of energy over long distances. In Fig. 3–3 above, we pointed out the average positions of long waves at 500-mb. These waves and those of small wavelengths move and change in amplitude. The high velocities in the jet stream can propagate the effects of these changes around the globe. Winds in the jet core sometimes are high enough to carry air, at latitudes of 40 to 50°N, around the earth in five days.

Mechanics of General Circulation

As noted earlier, the atmosphere may be regarded as a giant heat engine driven by solar energy. In Chapter 1 we discussed how solar energy is absorbed mostly at low latitudes and lost mostly at high latitudes through outgoing infrared radiation. The primary factor behind the general circulation is the temperature difference between equatorial and polar regions. At the same time, other factors are also of crucial importance in accounting for the pressure and wind patterns actually observed: the rotational speed of the Earth; the configurations of land and sea; and the physical and chemical properties of the air.

Certain aspects of the general circulation can be modeled with surprising similarity in laboratory experiments first performed by Dave Fultz at the University of Chicago in the late 1940's. The technique consists of using water to represent the air and a circular pan to represent the Earth. The pan is heated along the outside rim and cooled at the center where a circular cylinder is fastened. In this way the experiment simulates equatorial heating and polar cooling. The pan is rotated at varying speeds to simulate the Earth's rotation. Many other experimental variations can be introduced such as obstacles to represent mountains. Dyes are introduced into the liquid to serve as markers tracing fluid motions.

Laboratory studies such as these revealed many interesting and important results. They verified a discovery made earlier by the famous meteorologist, Carl-Gustav Rossby, that the character of fluid flow on a rotating body depends on the ratio of the characteristic velocity of the fluid to the characteristic velocity of the body. This quantity, known now as the *Rossby number*, for the Earth is about 0.1, i.e., the ratio of the speed of the jet stream (about 50 m sec^{-1}) to the speed of the Earth surface at the equator (about 500 m sec^{-1}).

When the dishpan experiment was performed at a Rossby number of about 0.1, the pattern of fluid motion (Fig. 3–5) was similar in many respects to the average motion in the free atmosphere shown in Fig. 3–4.

FIGURE 3–5 *Laboratory simulation of general circulation of the atmosphere. Courtesy Dave Fultz, Hydrodynamics Laboratory, University of Chicago.*

As might be expected, the fact that the dishpan is flat while the Earth is nearly spherical introduces difficulties. At the poles the Earth's surface is perpendicular to the axis of rotation as is the surface of the dishpan. As one goes toward the equator, the Earth's surface becomes more and more parallel to the axis, thereby reducing the effects of the rotation. This means that the pattern of flow in the real atmosphere at low latitudes has a larger Rossby number than 0.1. It also suggests that the rotation in the tropical atmosphere should be simulated by means of dishpan experiments at slow rotational speeds. This relation between latitude and speed was borne out by experiment.

These results indicate that the character of the general circulation, and particularly the separation of the tropical and middle-latitude atmosphere is closely coupled with the rate of rotation of the Earth. Herbert Riehl, an

Planetary patterns of air motion

authority on tropical meteorology, speculated that if the Earth's rotation were a half to a quarter of the present rate, the low latitude general circulation might reach as far as latitude 60° rather than the present 30°. Such considerations are of crucial importance in developing a notion of the atmospheric motions of other planets which rotate at speeds far different from those of the Earth.

Interactions of Air and Sea

The ocean has been called the thermostat of the Earth for reasons which are mostly obvious. The oceans represent a huge mass of a substance having a large heat capacity. They store an enormous quantity of energy and exchange it with the atmosphere. In winter the oceans serve to warm the cooler air moving over them. (See the maps in Fig. 7–2). In summer the ocean water tends to be cooler than surface air, and hence heat is transferred to the water.

The maps in Fig. 3–2 show the effects of land and ocean temperature differences on the surface pressure patterns over the Earth. These patterns, in turn, determine systems of weather and wind flow.

In prescribing the characteristics of the general circulation, the oceans are crucial not only as sources and sinks for heat, but as noted in Chapter 1, they are also the means by which large quantities of energy are transported from the warm equatorial regions to the colder polar regions. In this transport, they reduce the overall temperature difference and hence the driving force in the global wind system. The warm ocean currents such as the Gulf Stream, Kuroshio and Brazil Currents transport heat poleward, as the cooler waters such as the California and Peru Currents carry cold water equatorward.*

The ocean bodies of the world also affect the general circulation in ways which, in the past, have received little attention. One of these is associated with the upwelling of large quantities of cold water in the equatorial regions. This occurs in response to the deflection of surface water in opposite direction by the northeast and southeast trade winds. It has been reported that in the eastern Pacific, the upwelling water sometimes extends over regions several thousand miles across and are several degrees colder than the surrounding water. During certain years, there is no upwelling of cold water, and during others, bodies of low-temperature water appear suddenly. The well-known meteorologist Jakob Bjerknes, at U.C.L.A., has related the occurrence of large tongues of upwelling water to changes in the atmosphere circulation of the Northern Hemisphere.

*See K. K. Turekian, *Oceans*, Prentice-Hall, Inc., 1968.

Another prominent meteorologist, Jerome Namias, has observed that during some years, water temperatures in the North Pacific are as much as 6°C above the long term average. It has been speculated that such anomalies might exert control over the general circulation.

The degree to which the phenomena of sporadic, large-scale upwelling, or abnormal warming occur over the Earth's oceans still needs to be ascertained. Earth orbiting satellites equipped with appropriate radiometers should facilitate the detection and measurement of anomalies in ocean temperatures.

The interaction between sea and air can also be greatly influenced by the formation of sea ice. Joseph O. Fletcher, who has pioneered this subject, has noted that ice is a good insulator. In the Arctic, less than a meter of ice can maintain a temperature of the ice surface at −30°C while the ice is in contact with ocean water at −2°C. The ice effectively prevents the transfer of heat from water to air.

A second important role of ice is to increase the reflectivity of the surface. In summer, open polar oceans absorb about 90 percent of the insolation. This compares with the 30 to 40 percent presently absorbed by the highly reflective year-round ice.

The effect of the sea ice is therefore to suppress heat transfer from ocean to air and to reduce the quantity of absorbed solar energy. An increase in sea ice amplifies these effects leading to colder temperatures, more sea ice, and an extension of the same process. Once started it can continue until some other outside mechanism comes into play and reverses the process. Once the reverse process begins, it will also continue because of its positive feedback aspects.

How far the ice extension or elimination process must go on before it significantly influences the general circulation of the atmosphere still is not known. Records show that over past years, there have been great changes in the extent of the sea ice. For example, for about half a century ending in about 1940 there was a gradual warming of the Earth accompanied by a reduction of the extensions and thickness of the sea ice. In 1940, for reasons which still are not clear, the Earth began to cool and the process of sea-ice formation has reversed.

The Soviet climatologist, M. I. Budyko, predicted that if the Arctic pack ice were totally melted, the present incoming solar radiation would prevent it from reforming. Instead he visualized an ice-free Arctic Ocean and a different climatological region in the Arctic. One would also expect that the temperature difference between equatorial and polar regions would be smaller than at present, leading to major changes in the general circulation of the entire atmosphere. There still is considerable uncertainty about Budyko's hypothesis on an ice-free Arctic and the effects it would have on global circulation.

Planetary patterns of air motion

If the warming in the Arctic had continued beyond 1940 and gone on long enough to produce changes in deep ocean temperature, nature might have tested Budyko's hypothesis. Instead, there has been a general world-wide cooling and a growth of sea ice since the forties. As a result, it will be necessary to check the hypothesis by means of realistic theoretical models of the general circulation. Such a model might be used to predict how long and to what extent cooling will continue.

Theoretical Models of General Circulation

Earlier we discussed laboratory models of the general circulation. Although they have yielded new information, they still have some obvious limitations associated with difficulties in accurately simulating various important processes (such as cloud formation). Another promising approach to the study of the general circulation is through the medium of mathematical models. This is not a new idea, but it is one which was totally impractical until the development of large, high-speed electronic computers.

A mathematical model of the general circulation starts out with a number of equations which specifies the nature of the system and how it changes with time. A typical model consists of the following parts:

1. An equation of state relating pressure, temperature and density of the air.
2. An equation of motion relating changes with time in the three-dimensional air motions to the pressure and friction forces.
3. Thermodynamic equations dealing with temperature changes in the air-earth system.
4. Equations dealing with water vapor, clouds, and precipitation.
5. Equations dealing with the transfer of radiant energy through the atmosphere.
6. Equations dealing with heat and water balance at the Earth's surface.

The series of equations which describes this problem are interrelated and must be solved by numerical methods. This involves the specification of pressure, temperature, and humidity over a grid of points spaced perhaps 400 km apart horizontally. Conditions are followed at a number of pressure levels, sometimes as many as ten of them between 1,000 mb and 10 mb which include the altitude range from 30 km to about sea level.

In practice, when calculating the development of the general circulation, simple conditions are assumed to prevail at the outset. For example, it is sometimes assumed that the atmosphere is at rest and is isothermal, i.e., it has the same temperature everywhere. Then the Sun is "turned on" and all the processes incorporated in the mathematical model are allowed to function. During the first few "days" there is little motion as the equatorial regions get progressively warmer than the poles. When temperature differences become large enough, convection and three dimensional air motions begin. The effects of the Earth's rotation, sea-land differences, mountain ranges, cloud and rain formation, and other factors come into play. After about 200 to 300 model days, calculated general atmospheric circulations develop which have striking similarities to those actually observed (See Fig. 3–6).

FIGURE 3–6 *Computer-generated mean sea-level pressure in January: (A) computed and (B) observed. Isobars are at intervals of 4 mb and broken line is 1,000 mb. From Y. Mintz, A. Katayama, and A. Arakawa, University of California at Los Angeles, 1972.*

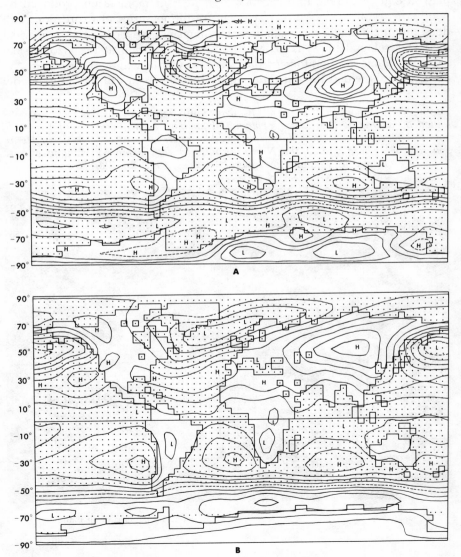

The models can not yet treat radiative transfers of energy in a satisfactory way. In particular, the effects of aerosols and certain trace gases still are not known adequately. To a certain extent, this is because of insufficient information about the quantities and characteristics of these substances.

Another major area of interest to the modelers is the interaction of sea and air. Since the two fluid systems are closely coupled, a change of temperature of one medium accompanies the change in the other. Mathematical models have been developed which take into consideration exchanges of radiant heat and turbulent transport of sensible heat as well as latent heat of vaporization. Water exchange by means of evaporation from the oceans and precipitation into the ocean are built into the model. Finally the mathematical equations take into account exchanges of momentum produced by wind stresses at the ocean surface. The resulting series of expressions still does not include all the exchange mechanisms. Neverthless a numerical model, developed by Syukuro Manabe and Kirk Brian at the Geophysical Fluid Dynamics Laboratory of the National Oceanic and Atmospheric Administration, yielded the encouraging results shown in Fig. 3–7. The model

FIGURE 3–7 *Computed pattern of mean temperature in degrees Celsius obtained by averaging the patterns calculated for both hemispheres around latitude zones. The right-hand side shows observed temperatures in the Northern Hemisphere atmosphere and in the North Atlantic Ocean. From S. Manabe and K. Bryan,* Journal of Atmospheric Sciences, *1969,* **26**: *786–789.*

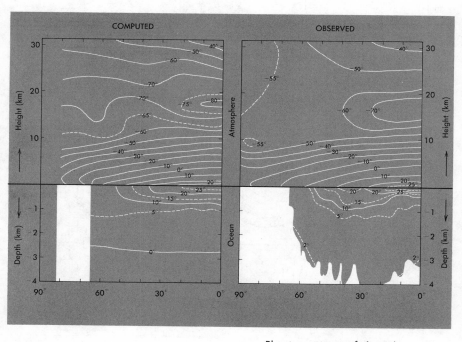

Planetary patterns of air motion

shows that the computed temperature structure in the atmosphere and oceans are in good agreement with observed conditions.

To give some notion of the role of the electronic computer in this type of research, it seems worth noting that the calculations which led to Fig. 3–7 required 1,200 hours of computation on the UNIVAC 1108.

It is clear that a great deal of progress has been made in developing theoretical models of the general circulation of the atmosphere and the interaction of atmosphere and oceans. These models offer the hope of making weather forecasts one to two weeks in the future. For this purpose more complete observations are needed of the Earth's atmosphere than are being obtained at present. There are large open spaces over the oceans, particularly over the Southern Hemisphere. Earth orbiting satellites offer the hope of supplying the needed observations. Many of the required measurements can already be made by means of remote sensors in orbit. By the end of the 1970's, we should see the establishment of the Global Atmospheric Research Program (abbreviated GARP), a massive international program devoted to the establishment of an adequate worldwide observational program and the development of improved models of the Earth's atmosphere.

Other Scales of Motion

The general circulation of the atmosphere is composed for the most part of broad air currents moving around the globe with relatively small northward and southward displacements in the form of a few very long waves. Within the general circulation there are many smaller scale perturbations of wind, pressure, and temperature which change fairly rapidly. These perturbations are associated with storm systems of various kinds.

On any weather map, you see centers of low pressure which often appear as patterns of nearly concentric, circular isobars. The closed wind circulation around such a center of low pressure is called a *cyclone*. A closed circulation of air around a region of high pressure is called an *anticyclone*. As noted in Chapter 2, in the Northern Hemisphere the winds blow counterclockwise around a cyclone, and clockwise around an anticyclone. The directions are reversed in the Southern Hemisphere.

Cyclones and anticyclones have diameters ranging from several hundred to several thousand kilometers and they may last for many days. Sometimes they evolve and move rapidly; other times they remain almost stationary. Generally, the winds near the ground in a typical cyclone or anticyclone are not strong; speeds of 5 to 10 m sec^{-1} are common. This is not true in cyclones forming over tropical oceans and developing into hurricanes. These storms, to be discussed in Chapter 6, sometimes have winds approaching 100 m sec^{-1}.

Planetary patterns of air motion

51

In the popular press, the name cyclones is sometimes given to tornadoes, the very violent short-lived storms which commonly have diameters of a few hundred meters and durations measured in minutes.*

The timing and intensity of the monsoon over India or of monsoonal circulations over other parts of the world are governed by the general circulation of the atmosphere. When improved techniques are developed which allow longer period predictions of the state of the atmosphere over the entire planet, it should be possible to make better predictions of the behavior of monsoonal circulations.

*The characteristics of cyclones, hurricanes, and tornadoes will be discussed in later chapters.

4

Fronts and cyclones

In Chapter 1, we noted how heat must be transported pole-ward in order to explain the observed temperature structure of the atmosphere. The atmospheric part of the transport mechanism is carried out in a number of ways. For the most part, in the tropics, there is a thermally driven convection circulation. Warm air rises over the intertropical conver-gence zone, moves poleward at high levels, sinks in the high pressure cells in the subtropics and completes the circula-tion as low-level trade winds blowing equatorward.

In middle latitudes, the poleward transfer of heat and moisture occurs mostly as a result of north and south mix-tures of warm and cold air. Large masses of warm, humid air from over the southern oceans move northward while cool bodies of air move southward in other nearby regions. Often the boundaries between the warm and cold air masses are quite sharp and easily identified. In such circumstances, they are called *fronts*.

As will be seen, many changes in day-to-day weather can be explained in terms of air masses and fronts.

Air Masses

Meteorologists use the term *air mass* to mean a widespread body of air whose properties are nearly homogeneous throughout its horizontal extent. In particular, in a given air mass one would expect only small differences in temperature and humidity from one point to another at the same level. For example, the temperature difference over a distance of 100 km would be small in comparison with the difference observed across the boundary between two different air masses. The area covered by a single air mass can be several thousand kilometers across.

An air mass develops its characteristic properties by remaining over a particular region for periods long enough to allow its vertical temperature and moisture distributions to reach equilibria with the underlying surface. How this comes about will become clearer as we examine the properties of the major air masses and see how they develop.

The most widely accepted system for classifying air masses, uses the thermal characteristics of the source regions: tropical (*T*), polar (*P*), and less frequently Arctic or Antarctic (*A*). The moisture characteristics of the air mass are represented by the words continental (*c*) and maritime (*m*) corresponding to dry and humid air respectively. In this classification, an air mass formed over a tropical ocean is called tropical maritime and labeled *mT*; a polar continental air mass, *cP*, is cold and dry and originates over a continental area at high latitudes.

When an air mass leaves its source region it gradually changes as a result of interactions with the underlying surface and vertical air motions. Air which is warmer than the surface it is passing over is identified by adding the letter *w*. Thus tropical maritime air moving over a cold continent is designated as *mTw*. When the air is colder than the underlying surface it is identified with the letter *k*. A polar continental air mass moving southward over warmer land is identified as *cPk*.

As noted in Chapter 2, the vertical stability of air depends mostly on how temperature varies with height. A *k* type air mass tends to be unstable because the warm surface produces a steep lapse rate and convection. As a result, the air generally is well mixed by vertical motions and therefore visibility through the air tends to be good. The daylight sky has a deep blue color when viewed through fresh, clear *cPk* air.

On the other hand, *w* type air masses will be stable near the ground because the air will be warmer than the cold surface. The resulting low-level temperature inversion will suppress vertical mixing. In such circumstances, air pollutants will be trapped and vertical mixing will be restricted. The suspended aerosols scatter sunlight in such a fashion as to give the sky a whitish cast.

The major source regions of various air masses affecting North America are shown in Fig. 4–1. As noted earlier, they are large areas having generally uniform surface conditions.

Polar continental air masses originate over the snow- and ice-covered land masses of Asia and North America. The chief processes in the formation of *cP* air are radiation and condensation. The white surface reflects much of the incoming solar rays and at the same time is an efficient emitter of heat in the form of infrared waves. The air close to the ground radiates heat both upward to the sky and downward to the snow surface which in turn radiates upward. Some of the energy is absorbed by the humid air, but some of the energy is lost to outer space. As a result the temperature of the air close to the ground decreases. The process continues as a deeper and deeper layer of cold, stable air is produced. When the temperature of the surface falls low enough, water vapor condenses on the ground. This re-

FIGURE 4–1   *Air mass source regions over North America.*

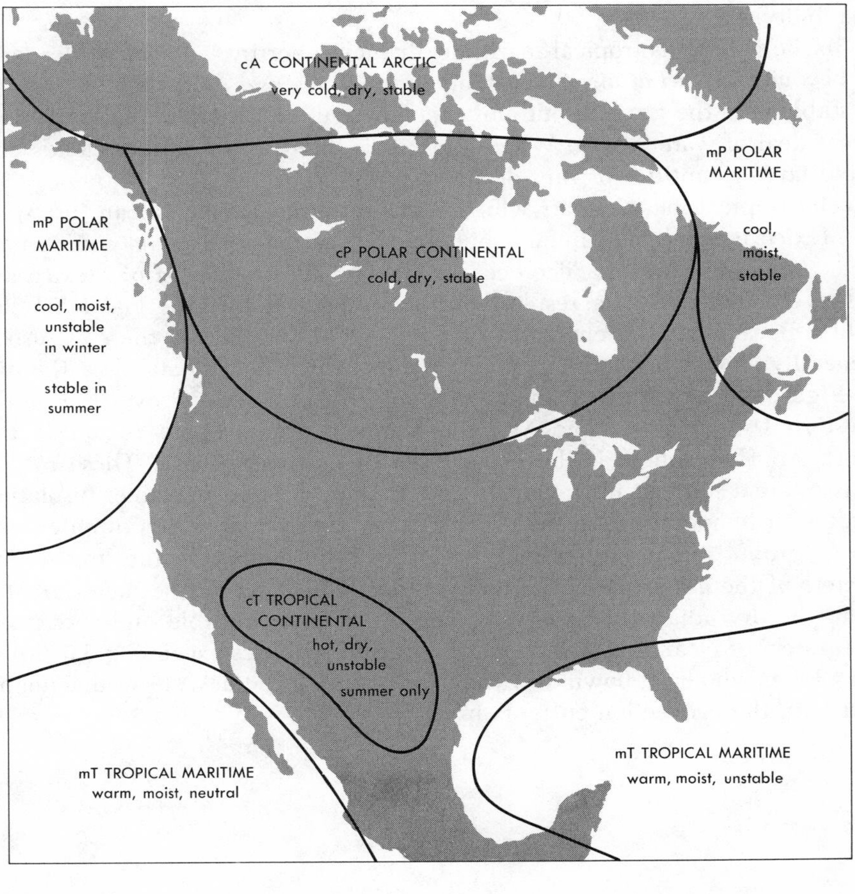

duces the water vapor content of the air and leads to the characteristic low humidity in *cP* air.

In some cases, the cooling process can go on for several weeks and produce a huge region of cold, dry air 2,000 to 3,000 meters deep.

Arctic air masses are an extreme form of polar continental air. They form over polar ice and are very cold and dry.

When a *cP* or *cA* air mass moves over the ocean in the winter, it can be converted to an *mP* air mass in only one or two days. The underlying water, having a higher temperature than the air, warms it by conduction. This leads to instability and convection currents which rapidly transport heat upward. The convection also transports water vapor evaporating from the sea surface into the dry air.

Most of the summer showers and thunderstorms over the United States develop in tropical maritime air from the Gulf of Mexico, the Caribbean Sea, and the nearby Atlantic Ocean. The ocean waters in these regions have relatively high temperatures and as a result they warm the air moving over them. At the same time, water vapor is evaporated into the air in large quantities. Convection mixes heat and water vapor vertically through the atmosphere. The chief properties of *mT* air are its high humidity and instability.

In the winter, as tropical maritime air moves northward over colder land it becomes an *mTw* air. Since temperature increases with height, the air is stable near the ground, but aloft, the air remains unstable and contains a great deal of water vapor. When such air is lifted, the resulting clouds can yield large quantities of rain or snow.

The tropical maritime air which forms over the Pacific Ocean just west of Mexico is warm and humid, but it is not as unstable as its counterpart over the Gulf of Mexico. The ocean waters off the west coast of Mexico are relatively cool and as a result there is a tendency towards low level stability. Because of the character of the general circulation, there is also a generally sinking air motion in this region which acts to stabilize the air.

Figure 4–1 also shows a source of tropical continental air over the southwestern United States and Mexico. A much larger source region in the Northern Hemisphere is the desert area of northern Africa. These *cT* air masses are a summer phenomenon and are hot, dry and unstable. Insolation causes air temperatures in the deserts to reach extremes which often exceed 40°C; ground temperatures may be 10 to 20°C higher. In the lowest few meters of the atmosphere, the temperature lapse rate can be much greater than the dry adiabatic lapse rate. The air is very unstable and there is a great deal of clear air convection, often up to altitudes exceeding 3,000 meters. Pilots who have flown over the deserts during the day are well acquainted with the convection currents in *cT* air.

Fronts

When two air masses of differing types encounter one another, they do not mix readily. Instead, the colder one slides under the warmer one and a transition zone develops between them. It is called a front because the concept was first discovered by Norwegian meteorologists during World War I when the newspapers spoke of such things as the "western front." Typically, a front is some 15 to 30 km wide.

The principal frontal system in the atmosphere separates the large body of polar air from the warmer tropical air. This boundary, called the *polar front*, sometimes extends with few interruptions around almost the entire Northern Hemisphere. As will be seen, many major storm systems are associated with the polar front.

Meteorologists classify fronts according to which air mass is advancing (Fig. 4–2). When cold air is advancing and pushing warm air ahead of it, the transition zone is called a cold front. Showers and thunderstorms often are formed in the warm air rising over a cold front's leading edge, particularly when the warm air is moist and unstable.

When warm air is advancing and forcing cold air to retreat, the boundary is called a warm front. It is shallower than a cold front with a slope rising perhaps 1 km over a distance of 200 km while a cold front might be twice as steep. The warm air gliding up a warm front sometimes contains widespread clouds, rain, and snow.

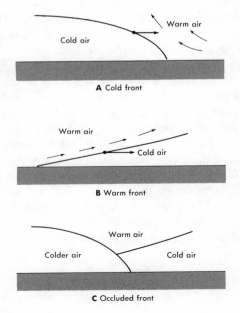

FIGURE 4–2 *Schematic drawing of vertical cross sections through (A) a cold front, (B) a warm front, and (C) an occluded front.*

If the boundary between warm and cold air does not move, it is called a stationary front. When a cold front overtakes a warm front, and underruns it, we say the fronts are *occluding*.

Since fronts separate air masses having quite different properties, it is clear that when forecasting the weather, it is helpful to keep track of frontal positions and predict their future behavior.

An examination of weather maps reveals that the task of explaining and predicting the weather requires more than merely tracking fronts. It is necessary to account for the formation of new fronts and the dissipation of old ones. Equally important, it is necessary to explain the occurrence of cyclones. They are the source of the major storm systems and most of the rain and snow in winter.

Cyclones

As long ago as the early part of the nineteenth century, it was recognized in England that large storm systems were associated with passing regions of low pressure. For about a hundred years, various scientists speculated about the properties of such cyclonic storms. Unfortunately, there was a paucity of reliable observations taken over a sufficiently large region. This made it difficult to construct a reasonably complete picture of what was happening in storm centers.

Major advances in the understanding of cyclones were made towards the end of World War I by the Norwegian meteorologists Vilhelm Bjerknes, his son Jakob, and associates. They collected sufficient synoptic observations to study the structure of a number of cyclones over Europe. The result of their analyses is the now famous *frontal theory of cyclones*. It was widely accepted for about three decades as an adequate explanation. More recently, new ideas have been advanced.

According to the Norwegian school, a cyclone forms along a nearly stationary front following a pattern often observed on weather maps. The sequence of events is shown in Fig. 4–3. A perturbation develops on the front when cold air is deflected southward and warm air is deflected northward. In this process, potential energy is converted to kinetic energy when cold, heavy air behind the front sinks while warm, humid air rises.

As the wave develops, condensation occurs in the warm, ascending air, clouds form, and precipitation may occur. At the apex of the wave, there is a fall in pressure which produces a wave cyclone containing a warm front and cold front. The latter advances faster than the former, and the sector of warm air becomes progressively smaller. The air motion around a Northern Hemisphere cyclone is counterclockwise, and wind speeds in the warm

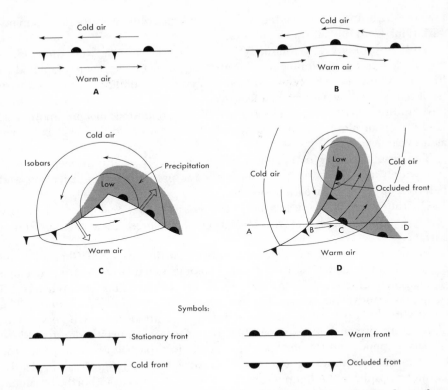

FIGURE 4–3 *Schematic representation of the formation of a wave cyclone along a frontal zone.*

sector exceed the speed of the warm front. As a result, the warm air rises over the cold wedge and may produce extensive cloud systems which will be discussed later.

Along the leading edge of the advancing cold front, there is a rapid rise of warm, humid air, and if the air is sufficiently unstable, thunderstorms are likely to occur.

As the cyclone continues to evolve the advancing cold front overtakes the warm front and occlusion occurs as shown in Fig. 4–3D. Under the occluded front there is a mixture of the cold air which was below both the cold and warm fronts. Continued occlusion leads to dissipation, and in the final stage, the cyclone is a weakening vortex composed of fairly uniform cold air.

In reality, the sequence of cyclone development may differ in many important details from the idealized pattern illustrated in Fig. 4–3. In particular the distribution of clouds and precipitation are often quite different from those depicted. Most of the weather is found ahead of the center of

Fronts and cyclones

low pressure and is associated with the warm front, but there are many variations from one storm to another.

The life cycle of a cyclone may last perhaps a day to a week depending on the degree of development. The first stages of development depicted in Fig. 4–3A and B may occur in hours. Typically, along a long stationary front many small wave disturbances occur, but only a small number of them develop into mature cyclonic storms. When one does occur, another is likely to occur along the same stationary front. This leads to what is known as a cyclone family.

The frontal theory of cyclones has been a very useful concept, and is still widely used by weather forecasters for predicting the formation and behavior of cyclonic weather systems.

On the other hand, it has not been possible to develop a satisfactory theoretical explanation for the formation of cyclones on a sloping frontal surface.

In the late 1940's, a number of scientists, particularly Jule Charney, now at the Massachusetts Institute of Technology, began investigating cyclone development starting from a different point of view. This research has led to a new concept known as the *baroclinic wave theory of cyclones*. The word baroclinic is used to specify a state of the atmosphere where surfaces of constant pressure are not parallel to surfaces of constant density. Since density depends mostly on the temperature, in a baroclinic atmosphere the temperature varies across a constant pressure surface (Fig. 4–4). Typically, in the troposphere the temperature decreases from south to north. In such a case, the north-south pressure gradient and the west-east wind velocity increase with altitude. When the wind increases markedly with altitude and other conditions are satisfied, baroclinic instability develops, and cyclonic storms may form.

FIGURE 4–4 *When the temperature and pressure surfaces are not parallel, the atmosphere is baroclinic and there is a tendency for circulations shown by the arrows. (When temperature and pressure surfaces are parallel, the atmosphere is barotropic.)*

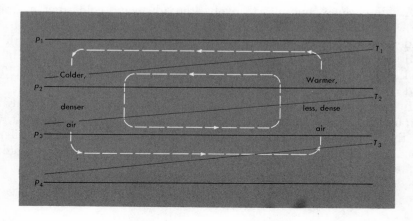

The baroclinic wave theory has a solid mathematical foundation in explaining the early stages of cyclone formation. It shows that for typical conditions in middle-latitudes with wind increasing with height, north-south perturbations in wind direction are sometimes unstable. In other words, once some perturbations are started, they increase in amplitude fairly rapidly.

The work of E. T. Eady about 1950 indicated that in typical circumstances when clouds and precipitation did not occur, the most unstable waves were long ones with lengths of about 4,000 km. They would double their amplitude, that is, the north-south excursions of the wind pattern, in about 40 hours.

The condensation of water vapor and release of latent heat in rising air has an important effect on the preferred wavelength and the time of development. Eady calculated that if the initial perturbation produced a region of clouds 5 by 150 km, wave cyclones having wavelengths of about 1,000 km would be the ones most likely to occur. Furthermore, storm amplitudes would double in about 14 hours. The calculated sizes and growth rates are in reasonable agreement with observations.

According to the baroclinic theory of cyclone development, the north-south perturbations of wind velocity are accompanied by vertical velocities. Where air is rising, there must be an inward flow of air to feed the updrafts. As the air converges, it develops a cyclonic spin at increasing speeds because of the effects of the Earth's rotation. According to the principle of the conservation of angular momentum, as the mass of a system gets closer to the axis of rotation the angular velocity increases. This is the same idea used by an ice skater when she brings her arms closer to her body in order to spin faster.

In areas of sinking air, the air diverges and its spin weakens; sometimes an anticyclonic circulation develops. This means a clockwise flow in the Northern Hemisphere and is associated with a high pressure region.

As a wave intensifies, the ascending current strengthens and causes more condensation and heat release. This in turn leads to still greater intensification and the concentration of the pressure falls in a small part of the disturbance. The consequence is a region of closed, nearly circular isobars which are characteristic of cyclones.

The baroclinic theory explains the formation of cyclones without reference to the existence of a frontal boundary between cold and warm air. One of the attractive features of the baroclinic theory is that it treats cyclones and anticyclones as an essential part of the general circulation. They form in the westerly flow in middle latitudes because other north-south exchange mechanisms are inadequate to transport energy northward. As the north-south temperature gradient increases, the middle latitude flow becomes unstable. It breaks down into cyclonic and anticyclonic waves which serve to transport heat poleward.

It should be noted that the baroclinic wave theory was developed through the use of mathematical techniques dealing with small perturbations in initial conditions. With the advent of high-speed computers and the development of numerical analysis methods, it has become possible to use theoretical models for the entire history of a cyclone. With some exceptions

FIGURE 4–5   *Operational numerical forecast of a surface pressure (millibars) pattern by means of a mathematical model. Courtesy F. G. Shuman and J. B. Hovermale, National Weather Service, NOAA. Note that the numerical model accurately predicted the rapidly developing cyclones over the Gulf of Alaska and over the eastern United States. The latter storm produced more than 30 cm of snow over the lower Great Lakes area. (A) Initial observed map was at 0700 EST on March 16, 1973.*

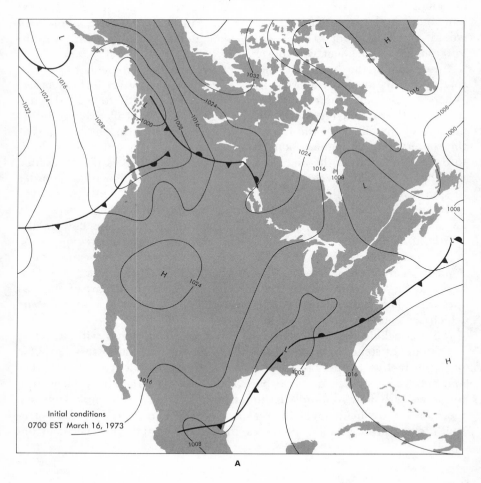

Initial conditions
0700 EST March 16, 1973

A

the approach is similar to the mathematical treatment of the general circulation mentioned in Chapter 3. For example, for periods up to several days, it is not necessary to take into account atmosphere-ocean interactions and the conditions over the entire Earth.

When considering the development of traveling cyclones and anticyclones in the Northern Hemisphere, you must write the equations of motion which relate accelerations of air velocities to pressure and friction forces on the rotating earth. In a complete model, equations must be included to take into account energy transfer by radiation and energy transformations through condensation and evaporation.

Since the equations specify changes with time of the state of the atmos-

FIGURE 4–5 *(B) Predicted pattern of surface pressure at 0700 EST on March 17 (the model does not predict fronts).*

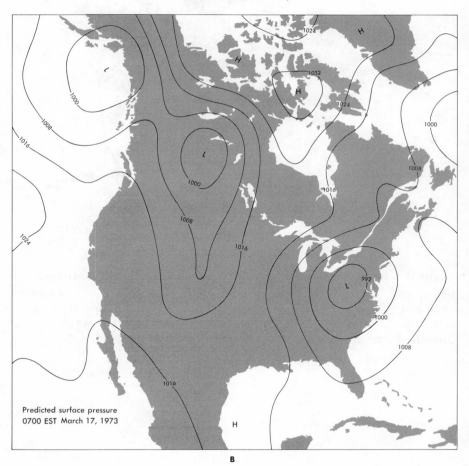

Predicted surface pressure
0700 EST March 17, 1973

B

Fronts and cyclones

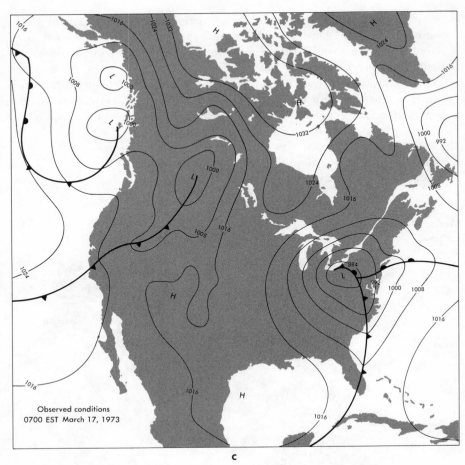

FIGURE 4–5 (C) Observed conditions at 0700 EST on March 17.

phere, it is necessary to know the initial weather conditions if accurate predictions of future conditions are to be made. There have been rapid advances in the development of numerical techniques for investigating the formation of storm systems. The success in predicting the formation and growth of cyclones over North America is illustrated in Fig. 4–5.

5

Clouds, precipitation, and

the hydrologic cycle

As everyone knows, there are many types of clouds. Some are flat, thin, and nearly transparent; others have the shape of cauliflowers and are brilliantly white; still others are dark ominous mounds and sometimes seem capped with a flat grey anvil. Some clouds yield rain or snow or are the source of strong winds, lightning and thunder, but most clouds go through their life cycles without any of these outward manifestations. The structure, appearance, and movement of a cloud depend on various properties of the atmosphere, particularly the vertical velocities of the air.

Composition of Clouds

Most clouds are composed of tiny spheres of water which grow by condensation in a rising body of air. The normal sequence of events is the following. When air ascends in the atmosphere, it moves to regions of progressively lower pressure. As a consequence, the air expands and cools (as noted in Chapter 2). Since the mass of water vapor in the rising air is unchanged, a reduction of the temperature leads to an increase in the relative humidity of the air. This results from the fact that the quantity of water vapor needed to saturate the air decreases as the temperature decreases.

The increase in humidity in an ascending volume of air also can be measured by noting the changes in air temperature and the *dew point* temperature of the air. The latter quantity gets its name from the fact that when the air temperature equals the dew point temperature, condensation begins.

If air remains at one level (e.g., the ground) and no water vapor is added to the air by evaporation, the dew point is reached by the air's cooling. This often is brought about by nightime radiation and results in the formation of dew on the cooled surfaces of grass, leaves and other objects.

If the saturation point is below freezing, the result is the formation of frost rather than dew. The temperature at which this occurs is called the *frost point*.

When a volume of air having a temperature, T and a dew point, T_D, is rising, both temperatures decrease. As noted in Chapter 2, T decreases at a rate of 1°C per 100 meters. The lapse rate of T_D is slower amounting to about 0.2°C per 100 m. Therefore, if a volume of air at sea level has values of T and T_D of 20°C and 12°C while rising, T will become equal to T_D at an altitude of 1,000 m. At this level the air will be saturated and condensation will begin on the surfaces of small particles in the air. In this way a cloud starts to form.

The minute particles in the air on which cloud droplets grow are called *condensation nuclei*. Typically, they have diameters of about 0.1 microns (0.00001 cm) or more and are found in concentrations of about 100 to 1,000 per cubic centimeter of air. As shown in Table 1–2, the atmosphere contains huge numbers of particles, but most of them are too small to be condensation nuclei at the humidities which occur in the atmosphere.

Nuclei come from many sources, particularly blowing soil, volcanoes, smoke stacks, and the oceans. In addition, nuclei are formed in the atmosphere as a result of chemical reactions involving gases such as sulfur dioxide and nitrogen dioxide. The most favorable nuclei are *hygroscopic*, that is, they have a marked ability to accelerate the condensation of water. Examples of hygroscopic nuclei are acid particles and sea salt. Condensation on ordinary table salt, sodium chloride, may begin when the relative humidity is only 75 percent. Magnesium chloride is even more hygroscopic, and condensation can start with relative humidities below 70 percent.

In an ascending current of saturated air, cloud droplets grow rapidly; in a few minutes they may have diameters of 5 to 10 microns. In a strong updraft, condensation cannot proceed as fast as water vapor is made available. As a result, the air becomes *supersaturated*. In this circumstance, the

FIGURE 5–1 *Photograph of cloud droplets captured on an oil-coated microscope slide. The largest ones are about 40 microns in diameter.*

relative humidity exceeds 100 percent and may get as high as 101 or 102 percent. Cloud droplets continue growing as long as the air is supersaturated.

In an ordinary cloud, droplets range in size from just a few microns up to perhaps 40 to 50 microns in diameter (Fig. 5–1). These sizes can be visualized by comparing them with the diameter of a human hair which is about 100 microns.

Although the droplets form on nuclei of some kind, the water making up the droplets is surprisingly pure because there is very much more water than nuclei material. For example, if a 50 micron drop formed in a 0.1 micron nucleus, the volume of water would be about 125,000,000 times greater than the volume of nuclei material.

The purity of water in clouds is important because it accounts for the fact that many clouds are composed of water droplets even when their temperatures fall below the nominal freezing point at 0°C. Such clouds are called *supercooled*. As will be seen later, supercooled clouds serve as the physical basis for many techniques of cloud and weather modification which employ cloud seeding.

Not all clouds are made up of water droplets. Most clouds found at altitudes where temperatures are below 0°C are composed of ice crystals. Even those clouds which initially are supercooled, generally are converted to ice by natural causes when they reach sufficiently low temperatures.

Extremely pure water can be supercooled to about −40°C. At lower temperatures, ice forms without the presence of foreign substances in the water. At higher temperatures especially at about −5 to −20°C, where ice crystals usually occur in the atmosphere, the ice formation is started by particles called *ice nuclei*. Table 5–1 lists the temperatures at which small particles of various substances produce ice crystals.

Natural ice nuclei are thought to come chiefly from the ground. Certain clays such as kaolinite and montmorillonite are abundant and reasonably effective nuclei because they initiate the ice process at temperatures between —9 and —16°C. As shown in Table 5–1, certain substances produce

Table 5–1

Threshold Temperatures at Which Various Substances Produce Ice Crystals

Substance	Temperature (°C)
Dry Ice	0
Silver iodide	—4
Lead iodide	—6
Naturally occurring	
Covellite	—5
Vaterite	—7
Magnetite	—8
Kaolinite	—9
Illite	—9
Haematite	—10
Dolomite	—14
Montmorillonite	—16

Source: B. J. Mason, *The Physics of Clouds*, Oxford Univ. Press, 1972.

ice crystals at warmer temperatures, but they are scarce in nature. Once ice crystals have formed in a cloud, the number can be increased by the splintering of existing crystals.

Crystals can take on a great variety of shapes depending mostly on the temperature and vapor pressure of the air (Fig. 5–2). A notable feature of ice crystals is their hexagonal construction which is attributed to the hexagonal structure of the H_2O molecule. Some crystals are long hexagonal columns, others are flat hexagonal plates. The most beautiful ones are the dendrites because they come in an infinite variety of patterns with intricate structures which are a pleasure to behold.

Cloud Types

Over the years, a number of procedures have been devised for classifying clouds. The most widely used classification was introduced by an English chemist, Luke Howard, in 1803 and is the one adopted by the World Meteorological Organization (WMO). For the most part, the clouds are classed according to their appearance. In the WMO system, there are ten cloud

Clouds, precipitation, and the hydrologic cycle

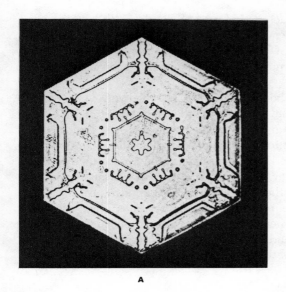

A

C

B

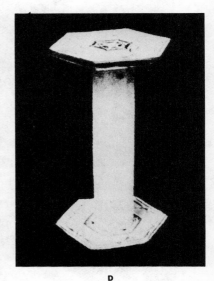

D

FIGURE 5–2 *Various types of ice crystals found in the atmosphere. (A) plate; (B) dendrite; (C) column; (D) column capped with plates. From W. A. Bentley and W. J. Humphreys,* Snow Crystals, Dover Publications, Inc., 1962.

Clouds, precipitation, and the hydrologic cycle

genera based on the main characteristic forms of clouds. Each of the genera comes in one or more of fourteen *species* depending on peculiarities in the shapes or internal structures of the clouds. In addition, they are further subdivided according to the arrangement of their parts, transparencies and other distinctive features.

There is little point, in this book, to go into a detailed discussion of the great variety of clouds. On the other hand, the characteristics of certain common ones deserve a few remarks. For most purposes, you can consider clouds to fall into three main groups: *cumulus, stratus,* and *cirrus.*

Cumulus are generally individual clouds having the appearance of rising mounds, domes, or towers. They are formed by convective currents whose structure can be visualized by the white, cauliflower appearance of the upper parts of the clouds. As a cumulus cloud enlarges, it is given the name *cumulus congestus.* Finally, when rain begins to fall it becomes a *cumulonimbus* (Fig. 5–3). Such a cloud often produces lightning and thunder and therefore is sometimes called a thundercloud or a thunderstorm.

FIGURE 5–3   *The development of a cumulonimbus cloud. Time is in hours and minutes.*

1356   MST †

1401   MST †

1406 MST ↑

1411 MST ↑

1416 MST ↑

FIGURE 5–3 (continued)

Stratus clouds, as the name implies, are those arranged in flat layers. When the cloud appears as a grey uniform sheet at an elevation below a kilometer or two, it is called stratus. If a cloud having this appearance occurs at higher altitudes, say 3 or 4 km, it is called *altostratus*. A stratified cloud yielding rain or snow is called *nimbostratus*.

When many cumuliform cloud elements are arranged in a layer and the cloud is below about 3 km with the elements appearing fairly large, the composite is called a *stratocumulus* (Fig. 5–4). If the cloud layer is between about 3 and 6 km, the individual elements appear relatively small, the cloud is called *altocumulus* (Fig. 5–5).

FIGURE 5–4 *Stratocumulus cloud. Courtesy U.S. Department of Commerce, NOAA.*

FIGURE 5–5 *Altocumulus cloud shaped like a giant lens and therefore called altocumulus lenticularis. Courtesy U.S. Department of Commerce, NOAA.*

FIGURE 5–6   *Cirrus cloud. Courtesy U.S. Department of Commerce, NOAA.*

Cirrus clouds are composed mostly of ice crystals and usually occur at high altitudes (Fig. 5–6). The clouds are often in the form of white, delicate filaments. When a cirroform cloud appears as a whitish veil which is fibrous or smooth and covers much or all of the sky, it is called *cirrostratus*. Such a cloud sometimes produces a *halo*, a circular ring of light which subtends an arc of 22 degrees with the sun or the moon at the center. Haloes are produced by refraction of light by ice crystals having the shape of hexagonal prisms. Sometimes haloes exhibit colorations ranging from red on the inside to blue on the outside.

Occasionally you see a high layer of clouds composed of many very small cloud elements having the appearance of grains or ripples (Fig. 5–7). Such *cirrocumulus* clouds often take on spectacular reddish colorations as the sun

FIGURE 5–7 *Cirrocumulus. Courtesy U.S. Department of Commerce, NOAA.*

Clouds, precipitation, and the hydrologic cycle

sets. The blue component of sunlight is scattered out of the rays as they pass through long distances of cloudless air containing a heavy loading of tiny aerosols. Sometimes cirrocumulus resemble the scales of a mackerel, and the phrase "mackerel sky" is used to describe the view.

Occasionally the sequence of clouds passing overhead is a good indication of the weather changes likely to occur during the next day or two. Long before the advent of government weather services, sailors and farmers used wind and cloud observations to predict the weather. Such observations are particularly informative during the approach of developing cyclones in the middle latitudes. The reasons for this are illustrated in Fig. 5–8 which shows a vertical cross section through a cyclone such as the one depicted in Fig. 4–4.

As the warm front approaches, the surface winds are generally from the southerly quadrant; high in the sky, cirrus clouds appear. The cirrus are slowly replaced with a layer of cirrostratus. It thickens, and lowers, and becomes altostratus as the surface warm front gets closer. Perhaps a day after the first sighting of the cirrus, rain or snow starts falling from the lowering overcast of thick nimbostratus clouds.

With the passage of a surface warm front, the winds shift abruptly to the southwest and temperatures rise. The sky clears gradually. Air in the warm sector may be quite humid. Sometimes scattered cumuliform clouds and cumulonimbus occur. The appearance of patches of altocumulus at high elevations signals the approach of a cold front. Organized bands of showers and thunderstorms often occur ahead of or along the surface cold front. When it passes, the wind shifts to the northwest, generally increases, and becomes gusty. Temperatures may fall rapidly and skies clear as cold, dry air passes over the point of observation.

FIGURE 5–8   *Clouds associated with a fully developed cyclone. This vertical cross section is taken along the line ABCD in Fig. 4–3D. Note that the horizontal and vertical scales are very different.*

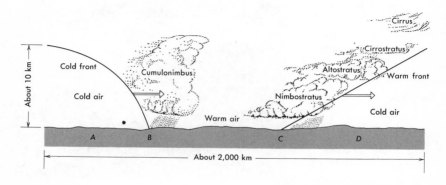

Clouds, precipitation, and the hydrologic cycle

If every cyclonic storm followed this simple pattern, weather forecasting would be easy. In fact, patterns of winds, clouds, and precipitation vary from storm to storm. In some cases, cyclones move rapidly and the sequence of weather events may take a day or two. In other cases, storms may stagnate over a particular region, and rain or snow may go on for nearly a week.

Formation of Rain, Snow, and Hail

Although condensation readily produces cloud droplets, in normal circumstances it can not produce raindrops. Once a cloud droplet reaches diameters of a few tens of microns, the water is so pure that condensation can continue only if the air is supersaturated with water vapor. But as the air approaches saturation, there are many small, relatively inactive condensation nuclei which can be activated. In such a circumstance the available water vapor is condensed on the smaller, newly formed droplets rather than the existing larger ones. As long as there are large numbers of condensation nuclei available, and this is almost always the case, the available water vapor condenses on so many particles that few exceed diameters of about 50 microns and most of them are much smaller. Raindrops usually are 10 to 100 times larger.

For many purposes, you can assume typical cloud droplet and raindrop diameters to be 20 microns and 2,000 microns (2 mm) respectively and typical concentrations of cloud and raindrops to be 100 droplets cm^{-3} and 100 drops m^{-3} respectively. Since the volume of a sphere is $(\pi/6)$ (D^3) where D is the diameter, the quantity of water in such a single raindrop is equivalent to the water in about a million such cloud droplets.

There are two principal mechanisms by which precipitation particles are produced in nature. The first one, called the *coalescence process*, involves the collision and merging of water droplets falling at different velocities. This occurs because the larger cloud droplets fall faster than the small ones (Table 5–2) and sometimes collide with them. The probability of collision depends on the relative sizes of the droplets. When there are some as large as 40 to 50 microns in diameter in a cloud composed mostly of droplets smaller than 20 microns, the frequency of collision is significant and increases as the larger drops grow.

Interestingly, laboratory experiments show that in some circumstances water droplets collide without coalescing. Instead, they bounce off one another. Apparently a very thin layer of air molecules prevents the water molecules from coming into contact, and surface tension forces give the droplets the elasticity allowing large deformations without breaking. Some experi-

Table 5–2

Fall Velocity of Water Drops in Still Air at Sea Level

	Diameter (Microns)	Fall Velocity (cm sec^{-1})
Cloud Droplets	1	0.004
	5	0.076
	10	0.30
	50	7.6
	100	30.
Raindrops	500	206.
	1,000	403.
	2,000	649.
	3,000	806.
	5,000	909.

Sources: R. J. List, *Smithsonian Meteorological Tables*. Sixth Ed., 1958. R. Gunn and G. D. Kinzer, *Journal of Meteor.*, 1949., Vol. 6, pp. 243–248.

ments have shown, however, that relatively small electric fields can cause essentially all collisions to be followed by coalescence.

There is no doubt that in relatively small convective clouds over the tropical oceans, rain is produced entirely by the coalescence process. Clouds having their bases at an altitude of about 600 m are often observed to rain when their tops reach 3 km where the temperature is about +7°C. The coalescence process also plays a part in the production of rain in many other clouds, but its importance is difficult to evaluate because some other process may also be at work.

Much of the Earth's precipitation falls in the form of snow or raindrops which come from melting snowflakes. An examination of snowflakes shows them to be large ice crystals or more commonly, aggregates of ice crystals. The process by which they form was studied in some detail about 1930 by the famous Scandanavian meteorologist Tor Bergeron and later extended by W. Findeisen in Germany. The so-called *ice-crystal process* is based on the condition that if ice crystals and supercooled water droplets exist at subfreezing temperatures, the crystals will grow while the droplets evaporate. This occurs because the saturation vapor pressure over water is greater than the saturation vapor pressure over ice at the same subfreezing temperature as shown in Fig. 5–9. As a result, there is a pressure force driving water molecules from water to ice.

As noted earlier, supercooled clouds often occur in the atmosphere. If

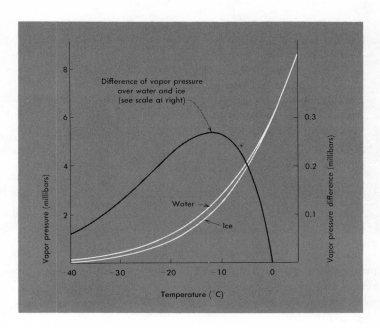

FIGURE 5–9 *Saturation vapor pressure over supercooled water and ice at the same subfreezing temperature (scale on left) and the difference between them (scale on right).*

ice crystals are introduced into such clouds, perhaps by the action of some effective ice nuclei, the stability of the cloud system is suddenly changed. The ice crystals grow rapidly as the water droplets evaporate. In some cases, the crystals reach diameters of a few hundred microns in a few minutes. As they grow, they begin falling through the cloud and colliding with supercooled droplets and other ice crystals. The droplets may freeze on contact and the crystals stick to one another. In this way, snowflakes may be produced.

If air temperatures are low enough, the snowflakes may reach the ground. On many occasions, however, the air near the ground has temperatures high enough above freezing to allow the snowflakes to melt and as a result rain occurs. In mountainous areas, it is common to see snow at the high elevations and rain in the valleys.

In some winter storms, strong temperature inversions occur in the lowest kilometer or two of the atmosphere and may lead to a particularly hazardous form of rain (Fig. 5–10). The snowflakes may melt as they fall through the warm layer having a temperature greater than 0°C. The water drops then become supercooled as they pass through the cold air. On striking the cold ground and other objects such as automobiles, trees and power lines,

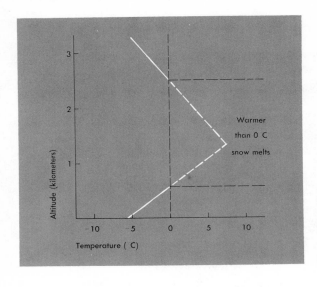

FIGURE 5–10 *Snowflakes melt as they fall through the warm layer where temperatures exceed 0°C. As liquid raindrops descend through the layer of subfreezing air near the ground, they may become supercooled and freeze on impact with the cold ground.*

the supercooled water freezes rapidly. This *freezing rain* coats everything with layers of hard, solid ice called *glaze*. The accumulated ice may cause widespread damage to vegetation and cause very dangerous driving conditions (Fig. 5–11).

When falling ice crystals encounter large quantities of supercooled drops,

FIGURE 5–11 *The effects of freezing rain. Courtesy U.S. Department of Commerce, National Oceanic and Atmospheric Administration, and New York Power and Light Co.*

the resulting frozen particles may have the form of a small *ice pellet*. These may also occur when supercooled raindrops freeze.

In a cumulonimbus cloud having a strong updraft and a large supply of supercooled water, ice pellets may become hailstones. On rare occasions they reach almost unbelievable sizes (as large as an orange) and are characterized by alternate layers of nearly transparent and milky ice. In order to explain the occurrence of these stones, it is necessary to find mechanisms by which the stone is maintained in a supercooled cloud for a substantial period of time. More will be said about this subject in the next chapter.

The Hydrologic Cycle

Since life on the Earth depends so crucially on an adequate supply of water, Earth scientists have given much attention to the exchanges and transformation of the water medium between atmosphere, oceans, and continents. The composite picture is called the *hydrologic cycle* (Fig. 5–12).

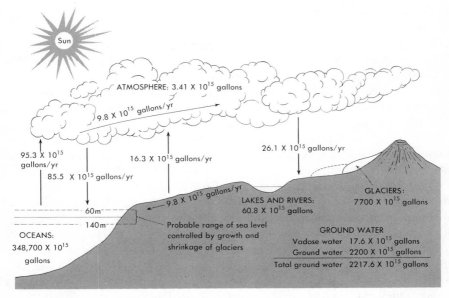

FIGURE 5–12   *The hydrosphere and hydrologic cycle. From B. J. Skinner,* Earth Resources, *Prentice-Hall, 1969.*

Although there is a great deal of water on the Earth, most of it is heavily loaded with salts and is contained in the oceans. This is shown in Table 5–3.

Clouds, precipitation, and the hydrologic cycle

Table 5-3

Estimates of Terrestrial Water

	Water Volume (gallons)	Percent of Total Water
Oceans	3.49×10^{20}	97.2
Continents		
Icecaps and glaciers	7.7×10^{18}	2.15
Ground water	2.2×10^{18}	0.62
Fresh water lakes	3.3×10^{16}	0.009
Saline lakes and inland seas	2.8×10^{16}	0.008
Vadose water (including soil		
moisture)	1.8×10^{16}	0.005
Average in stream channels	3.0×10^{14}	0.0001
Atmosphere	3.4×10^{15}	0.001
Totals	3.6×10^{20}	

Source: B. J. Skinner, *Earth Resources*, Prentice-Hall, 1969.

As far as human beings are concerned, the most vital water supplies are the relatively small quantities contained in rivers, lakes, ground water and which circulate between the atmosphere and the continents.

In this chapter, we have dealt with a part of the hydrologic cycle—the formation of clouds and precipitation. In Chapter 1, another part of the picture, namely evaporation from the oceans, was examined. A complete treatment of this subject could occupy an entire volume, but space permits only a brief outline of certain important points.

The hydrologic cycle traces and accounts for water as it enters the atmosphere as a result of evaporation, mostly from the oceans, but also from lakes, rivers, wet soil, and of transpiration from plants (See Fig. 5–12).

Over the entire Earth the quantity of water added to the atmosphere in an average year amounts to a depth of about 100 cm. This figure can be obtained from the data in Table 5–4 since oceans cover about 70 percent of the surface of the earth (0.70×125 cm yr^{-1} + 0.30×41 cm yr^{-1} = 100 cm yr^{-1}). As shown in Fig. 5–13, most evaporation occurs in the warm equatorial and tropical regions, particularly along latitude circles of about 20° north and south. These are the belts of the semipermanent anticyclones within which subsidence carries warm, dry air downward.

The water vapor in the atmosphere is transported upwards by turbulent motions and convective currents and carried long distances by the winds. When sufficiently strong and persistent updrafts occur, clouds and precipitation may occur. As a result, the water returns to the Earth's surface. Since the average quantity of water vapor retained in the atmosphere

Clouds, precipitation, and the hydrologic cycle

Table 5–4

Annual Water Balance of the Oceans and Continents in Centimeters per Year

Oceans	Evaporation E	Precipitation P	Total Runoff TR
Atlantic Ocean	104	78	—26
Indian Ocean	138	101	—37
Pacific Ocean	114	121	7
Arctic Ocean	12	24	12
All Oceans	125	112	—13
Continents	**E**	**P**	**TR**
Europe	36	60	24
Asia	39	61	22
North America	40	67	27
(United States)	56	76	20
South America	86	135	49
Africa	51	67	16
Australia	41	47	6
Antarctica	0	3	3
All Continents	41	72	31

Source: W. Sellers, *Physical Climatology*, Univ. of Chicago Press, 1965.

changes little, the annual average precipitation over the Earth must equal the evaporation. Therefore, the annual average rainfall equals about 100 cm, a quantity which greatly exceeds the depth of water vapor in the atmosphere at any time.

On the average, if all the water vapor in a vertical column of air extending from the ground to the top of the atmosphere were condensed, it would yield a layer of water about 3 cm deep. Since about 100 cm of precipitation falls in 365 days, the average planetary precipitation is about 0.27 cm day^{-1}. At this rate, the 3 cm of water vapor in the atmosphere would require 11 days to fall out. This is known as the *average turnover* or *residence* time of water vapor in the atmosphere. It indicates that water vapor entering the atmosphere in one place is likely to fall out over regions far from its source, because over an eleven day period, the winds will carry the water vapor over great distances.

The latitudinal distribution of precipitation over the entire Earth is shown in Fig. 5–13. As expected, there is a pronounced peak over the equatorial regions where there are frequent thunderstorms associated with the intertropical convergence zone. Precipitation minima are associated with the sinking air in the subtropical anticyclones between latitudes 20°–30°.

Clouds, precipitation, and the hydrologic cycle

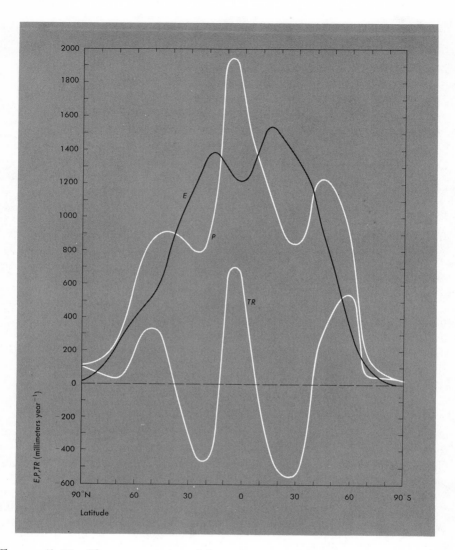

FIGURE 5–13 *The average annual latitudinal distribution of evaporation (E),
precipitation (P) and total runoff (TR). From W. D. Sellers,* Physical Climatology,
University of Chicago Press, 1965.

Secondary precipitation maxima at middle latitudes are largely attributed
to traveling cyclonic storms.

As seen in Table 5–4 and Fig. 5–2, more precipitation occurs over the
oceans than over the land. Again recalling that the oceans occupy about
70 percent of the surface area of the earth, it is found that only about 21
percent of all rain and snow falls on the continents. Some of it wets the
ground and vegetation and then evaporates again. Some of the water runs
off the continents in rivers and streams and returns to the oceans. Also a

small fraction percolates into the ground to recharge the aquifers and flow through the soil and rocks.

The difference between precipitation and evaporation is called the total runoff (TR) and is shown in Fig. 5–13 and Table 5–4. A negative TR means that evaporation exceeds precipitation, and excesses in some places must supply the deficits in others to maintain a long term balance. For example, over the Arctic Ocean, precipitation exceeds evaporation and excess water flows into the Atlantic to make up the precipitation deficit. Over all the continents, particularly South America, precipitation exceeds evaporation, and the total runoff balances the overall deficit of precipitation over the oceans. Note that the difference between 0.70×13 cm and 0.30×31 cm can be regarded as negligibly small when uncertainties in the estimates are taken into account.

It should be kept in mind that the quantities given in this section apply to averages over the Earth as a whole. They imply a degree of consistency which is probably obtained over periods of several decades. As will be seen in a later chapter, over perhaps half a century there can be important changes in the Earth's temperature accompanied by changes in the general circulation and in the quantity of water contained in sea ice and glaciers. At the same time, there would be vital changes in the hydrologic cycle. Since the supply of fresh water plays such a crucial role in human affairs, it is necessary to examine the degree to which the planetary water balance varies as the climate changes and to learn if human activities have any effect on the climate.

Severe storms

Weather systems which produce clouds, precipitation, and sometimes strong, gusty winds can be called storms. Most of them do much more good than harm. They yield rain or snow to water growing vegetation, to fill lakes and reservoirs with fresh water needed for a great many human activities.

Unfortunately, certain storm systems can also do a great deal of harm. For example, an intense winter storm can produce extreme subfreezing temperatures, deep snow, and strong winds. When such blizzards occur, they can be disastrous to man and beast. Grazing animals can become isolated and starve or freeze to death. Entire communities can be shut off from essential supplies.

Severe winter storms at least have the redeeming features that they can be forecast with a reasonable degree of accuracy and they move relatively slowly. In most cases steps can be taken to reduce the loss of life, particularly human life.

Certain storm systems, on the other hand, develop so rapidly and are so small and short-lived that they are difficult to predict accurately. The best examples are violent hailstorms and tornadoes, which sometimes strike with frightening speed. In a matter of minutes a hailstorm may destroy a field of corn, and a tornado may demolish a score of buildings leaving wounded and dead in its wake.

Still another type of severe storm is the hurricane and its counterparts in other parts of the world. These intense tropical storms, though not containing the concentrated energy of a tornado, are larger, longer-lived, can do much more damage to property, and cause more fatalities.

In this chapter we will examine some of the properties of thunderstorms, tornadoes, and hurricanes, which are all severe storms in which convection plays an important role.

Thunderstorms

As was noted in Chapter 2, when the temperature decreases rapidly with height and the air is humid, the atmosphere is unstable. These conditions are most commonly encountered in maritime tropical air. When a sufficiently large volume of such air is given an initial upwards velocity—by an advancing front or an orographic barrier, for example—a convective current is set in motion. As the air rises it accelerates because it will be warmer than its environment. When condensation begins and the latent heat of vaporization is released, the added buoyancy will supply added acceleration to the updraft. As the air continues ascending, the size of the cloud increases.

The depth of a convective cloud depends on the temperature lapse rate, the humidity of the atmosphere, and the size of the rising volume of air. If there is a temperature inversion aloft, it may act as a stable barrier preventing further convection. In some circumstances the updraft accelerates until it reaches the stable layer at the base of the stratosphere at altitudes as high as about 15 km. More commonly, thunderstorms extend to altitudes of about 10 km and often are topped by anvil clouds composed of ice crystals, blowing out of, and away from, the main cloud core.

Although thunderstorms take on many sizes, shapes and structures, they may be considered to fall into two broad categories: local or air mass thunderstorms and organized thunderstorms.

Local storms are best typified by fairly isolated storms having a short life time—less than an hour or so. They were studied in detail in the late 1940's by the Thunderstorm Project under the direction of the renowned meteorologist Horace R. Byers. On the basis of airplane penetrations, radar observations and other measurements, it was proposed that such thunderstorms are composed of one or more "cells" which follow a three-stage life cycle represented schematically in Fig. 6–1.

Severe storms

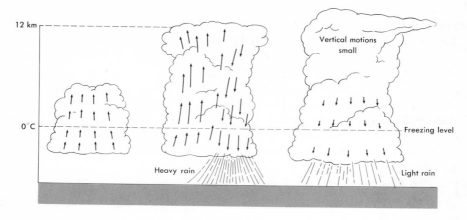

FIGURE 6–1   *The cumulus, mature, and dissipating stages in the life of a single cell thunderstorm. Based on H. R. Byers and R. R. Braham, Jr.*, The Thunderstorm, 1949.

In the cumulus stage, the cloud is dominated by updrafts and contains growing cloud and precipitation particles. As the cloud enlarges, the updrafts become stronger and more widespread. In the upper parts of the cloud where the buoyancy is small and large quantities of liquid water and ice exist, a downdraft is initiated. It spreads downward and horizontally through the cloud; at maturity the cloud contains updrafts and downdrafts. During this period, heavy rain occurs at the ground. In the final stage, the cloud is characterized by weak downdrafts and light rain.

Under the cloud, starting even before rain reaches the ground, downdraft air encounters the ground and spreads rapidly outward. The air originating high in the cloud is cool and moist, and depending on the strength of the upper level winds and the downdraft, can be blowing at a high velocity and be very gusty. It advances ahead of the thunderstorm, sometimes at speeds exceeding 30 m sec^{-1}, and is capable of doing a great deal of damage to vegetation and buildings.

Inside the cloud, updrafts and downdrafts can be quite strong and turbulent as any airline pilot can attest. An updraft as strong as about 25 m sec^{-1} was measured by a Thunderstorm Project airplane flying through a storm at about 5 km, but stronger draft speeds have been measured and calculated.

Although some small isolated thunderstorms, particularly over the dry western United States generate so little rain that it evaporates before reaching the ground, most local thunderstorms produce enough rain to water the crops and cool a hot summer day. Except for the occasional destructive out-blowing winds under the storm, the only other thing to fear is lightning.

Severe storms

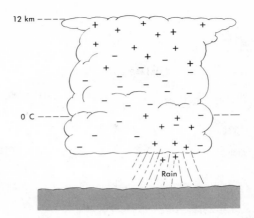

FIGURE 6–2 *Schematic representation of the electric charge distribution in a mature thunderstorm.*

As we have known since the days of Benjamin Franklin, lightning is a giant electrical discharge. Over the last couple of hundred years we have learned a great deal about thunderstorm electricity and lightning, but certain crucial questions still remain without satisfactory answers. It is now well accepted, as shown schematically in Fig. 6–2, that the upper part of a thunderstorm is predominantly positive while the lower part is mostly negative. A smaller positively charged center is often found in the rain region near the ground.

Surprisingly, there still is much debate among the experts about the principal mechanism by which the electrical charge is separated in a thunderstorm. Most authorities believe, on the basis of laboratory experiments and field observations, that the separation occurs as a result of interactions between ice particles and supercooled water drops. On the other hand, a small group of scientists believe that the charge is separated by the selective capture and transport by cloud droplets of tiny positive and negative ions in the atmosphere.

Organized Thunderstorms

When a thunderstorm or a group of them is said to be organized, there is an implication that it is longer lasting than typical local storms. In fact some meteorologists have used the term "quasi-steady state" to suggest only slow changes in the properties of the storm.

Most often the storms regarded as being in the organized class are those which form in lines or bands of thunderstorms, sometimes called "squall lines." They often are initiated along a cold front or ahead of and nearly

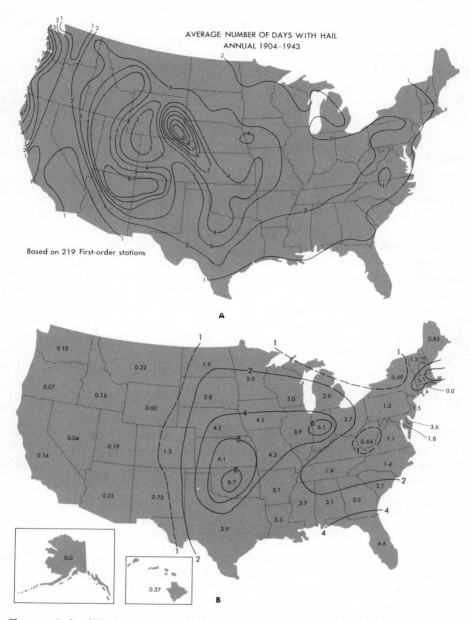

FIGURE 6–3 *(A) Average number of days with hail during period 1904–1943. Reports along west coast are more properly considered to be ice pellets and generally are no greater than 5 mm in diameter. From: Hydrometeorological Report No. 5, U.S. Weather Bureau, 1947. (B) Average annual number of tornadoes per 10,000 square miles based on state averages for the years 1953–1970. Source: National Weather Service.*

Severe storms

parallel to it. The lines of thunderstorms travel through the warm sector of cyclones at speeds often exceeding the speed of the cold fronts. Along the way the storms may deposit long swaths of hail and at times produce tornadoes.

The maps in Fig. 6–3 show the annual frequencies of these phenomena over the United States and are a measure of relative frequency of severe organized thunderstorms.

Various physical models of organized thunderstorms have been constructed. Unfortunately, most of them are based on limited observations. One of the best known models is shown in Fig. 6–4. The drawing shows air motions with respect to a storm which has developed in an environment where the westerly winds increase with height. Air enters the storm from the front and follows an upward sloping path. Clouds and precipitation particles form and grow in the updraft. Small ice particles are found in the upper, supercooled part of the cloud. Some of them fall out as rain or small hail. Others are carried upward and forward in the cloud and then fall back into the updraft and pass again through the region of supercooled water where they grow larger. Some hailstones can make several passages through the updraft, growing larger each time, until they become too large to be supported by the updraft and fall out of the cloud.

This model apparently can explain the occurrence of large hailstones—the stronger and more persistent the updraft, the larger the stones may be-

FIGURE 6–4 *Simplified version of the physical model of severe hailstorm proposed by Keith A. Browning and Frank A. Ludlam at Imperial College in London. Arrows show air movement with respect to the cloud.*

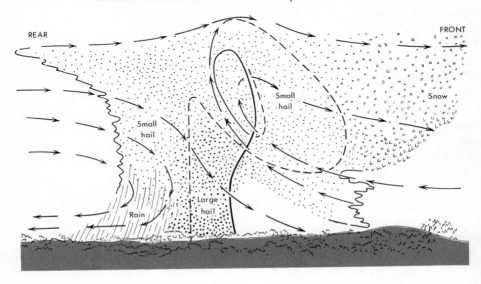

Severe storms

A

B

FIGURE 6–5 *(A) Thin slice cut from a large hailstone 4.5 cm in diameter and photographed by passing polarized light through the ice. This procedure reveals individual ice crystals in the hailstones. The regions of small ice crystals corresponds to milky ice; the regions of large crystals are clear ice. Courtesy Vincent J. Schaefer, State University of New York at Albany. (B) Thin slice through another hailstone about 4.5 cm in diameter viewed under ordinary light. Courtesy R. Schleusener, South Dakota School of Mines and Technology.*

come. The characteristic layers of clear and milky ice found in hailstones is also explained by the model in Fig. 6–5. When passing through a region with a heavy concentration of supercooled water, the hailstone accumulates more water than can be frozen quickly. The stone becomes coated with a layer of slowly freezing water and as a result mostly clear ice is formed. But when the hailstone passes through the upper parts of the cloud with small quantities of supercooled water, the colliding droplets freeze rapidly. This traps air bubbles in the ice and gives it a milky appearance.

Although the Browning-Ludlum model sketched in Fig. 6–4 has some appealing features, it does not adequately conform with many hail-producing thunderstorms and still does not have a satisfactory mathematical model to support it. At this point, it is fair to say that a great deal still needs to be learned about thunderstorms, particularly the large, severe traveling storms.

Tornadoes

Tornadoes are probably the most feared of all weather phenomena because of their concentrated destructive power. As shown in Fig. 6–6, they usually have the appearance of a narrow funnel, cylinder, or rope extending

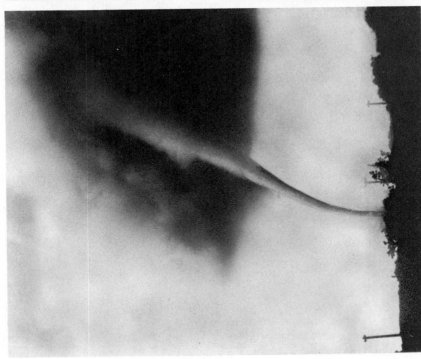

FIGURE 6–6 Photographs of two tornadoes. Courtesy U.S. Department of Commerce, NOAA.

Severe storms

from the base of a thunderstorm to the ground. The visible funnel is composed of water droplets formed by condensation in the funnel.

Tornadoes are typically less than a few 100 m in diameter, but some are much larger. The funnels usually touch the ground for only a few minutes or so, but some have been reported to last much longer. Maximum wind speeds are estimated to reach about 150 m sec.$^{-1}$ At one time it was thought, on the basis of the damage done, that tornado wind speeds were much higher, possibly even reaching the speed of sound.

The pressure in a tornado funnel is substantially lower than the surrounding atmospheric pressure. Measurements are scarce, but it has been estimated that, in a severe tornado, the central pressure might be about 100 mb less than the pressure in the environment.

The low pressure and strong winds account for the destructive nature of a tornado. When one of them moves over a building, the outside pressure suddenly drops while the pressure inside changes slowly, particularly if the windows and doors are closed. The result is a great pressure force which can cause the roof and walls to blow outward with explosive violence. Even very heavy objects can be picked up and moved by the powerful winds. Railroad cars and houses have been moved while remnants of demolished buildings have been scattered long distances.

In about 1970, T. T. Fujita, an authority on tornadoes, concluded that within a tornado there are still smaller, intense vortices that he called "suction spots." He suggested that they are the cause of much tornado destruction.

Another interesting aspect of tornadoes is the loud, distinctive noises they produce. People who have had the misfortune to have one pass near by have reported sounds resembling "a thousand railway trains" or "the roar of flights of jet airplanes." An adequate explanation has still not been obtained.

Although almost all tornadoes are associated with thunderstorms, meteorologists still do not agree on the relationship between them. As shown in Table 1–3, a tornado contains much less energy than a thunderstorm, and thus it is reasonable to suppose that the thunderstorm causes the funnel and supplies its energy. It has been speculated that electrical discharges might initiate and maintain the funnel but this idea does not have many supporters. Nevertheless, there is evidence that at least some tornadoes are electrically active.

Although tornadoes occur in many other countries, the United States experiences by far the highest frequency. In an average year there may be perhaps 700 separate tornadoes reported. Commonly a single large thunderstorm system will produce several tornadoes. In an intense outbreak as many as 30 or 40 separate funnels will be generated as the parent storm travels over distances of several hundred kilometers.

Severe storms

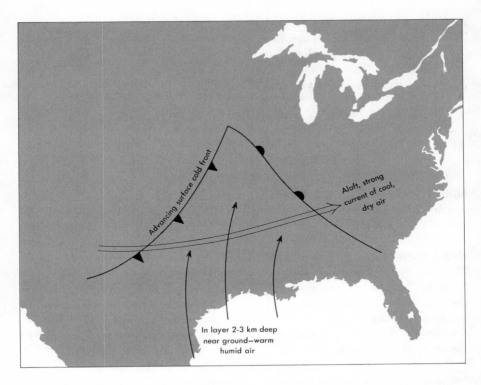

FIGURE 6–7 *Meteorological conditions favoring the formation of severe thunder-storms and tornadoes over the southern Great Plains.*

Tornadoes are most frequent in the late afternoon and early evening and occur most often in the spring and early summer months. It is during this period that the necessary meteorological conditions are most likely. Figure 6–7 illustrates circumstances in which tornadoes are common. A current of moist tropical air from the Gulf of Mexico sweeps over the Southern Great Plains. Aloft, a current of dry air from over the desert Southwest sweeps over the moist air. The advancing cold front initiates the lifting of the moist air and leads to convection. In the warm sector of the cyclone, thunderstorms are a common event. If the air is very unstable an intense squall line with tornadoes will be likely to develop.

Unfortunately it is not possible to pinpoint the region of tornado occurrence. Weather forecasters delineate areas, perhaps a couple of hundred kilometers across, within which severe thunderstorms and tornadoes are most likely. Radar sets are used to detect tornado-producing storms and to track them when they have been identified. As of the middle 1970's, the only certain way to identify a tornado is to observe it visually. Once one of them

Severe storms

has been sighted its parent thunderstorm can be followed by means of radar, and people in its path can be warned to seek cover or evacuate quickly.

There are conditions other than those depicted in Fig. 6–7 under which tornadoes come into being. One fairly common setting is within the already dangerous weather associated with a hurricane.

Hurricanes

The name hurricane is given to a tropical cyclone occurring over the Atlantic or the eastern North Pacific Ocean and having maximum wind speeds greater than 32.4 sec^{-1} (73 mph). The same type of storm in the western North Pacific is called a typhoon and in the Indian Ocean is called a cyclone. Various other names are used in other parts of the world. Figure 6–8 shows areas where they are observed and the tracks they commonly follow. For convenience, we shall call them all hurricanes.

As in the case with tornadoes, the chief characteristics of hurricanes are the low central pressure and the high wind speeds. But the two storms differ greatly in size and duration. A typical hurricane is a nearly circular vortex some 500 km in diameter which lasts for many days. Some storms last for more than a week.

The central pressure in a hurricane may be more than 50 mb lower than the pressure at the outskirts of the vortex and in a severe storm the pressure difference could be 100 mb. Since the pressure increases markedly with distance outward from the center, there are steep pressure gradients and high wind velocities (Fig. 6–9). Peak winds, sometimes exceeding 80 m sec^{-1} (180 mph) occur, usually within about 30 km of the storm center.

FIGURE 6–8 *Regions of the world where hurricanes form and the most common tracks they follow. From G. E. Dunn and B. I. Miller,* Atlantic Hurricanes, *Louisiana State University Press, 1960.*

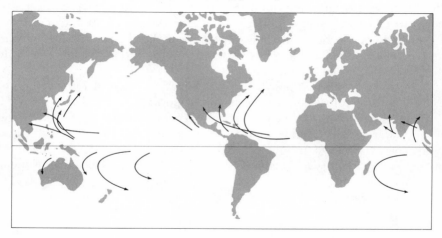

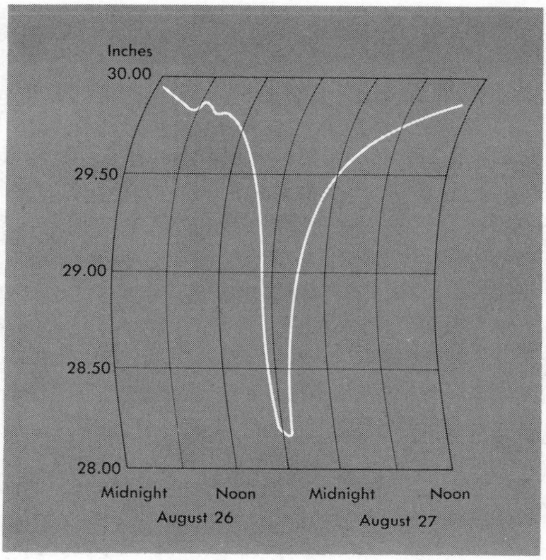

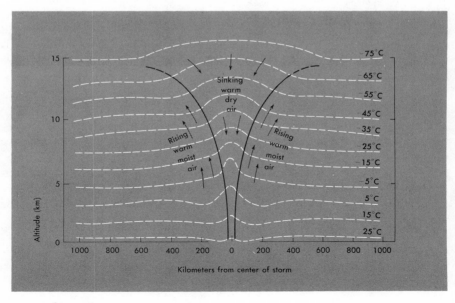

FIGURE 6–9 *The changes in pressure (in inches of mercury) as a hurricane passed West Palm Beach, Florida in August, 1949. (Note that 1 in. Hg = 33.9 mb = 0.49 lb in⁻²). From R. T. Zoch, Monthly Weather Review, 1949, 77: 339–341.*

In the innermost 20 km of the storm the winds are light and the sky contains few clouds. This is called the "eye" of the storm. In some very large storms, the eye may be more than 40 km in diameter.

A schematic cross section through a hurricane is shown in Fig. 6–10. The air in the interior part of the storm sinks, is dry and warmer than the air

FIGURE 6–10 *Schematic cross section showing temperature distribution and air motions in a mature hurricane. The heavy solid lines show the boundaries of the eye. Based on a model by E. Palmén, Geophysica (Helsinki), 1948, 3: 26–38.*

Severe storms

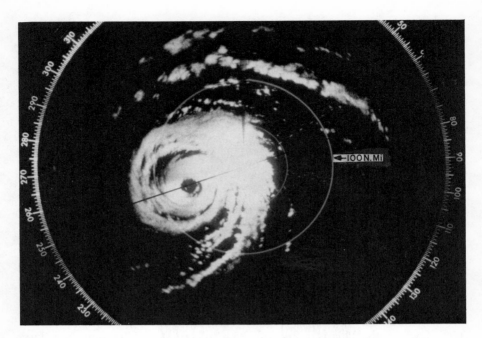

FIGURE 6–11 *Hurricane Donna at 7:30 A.M. EST on September 10, 1960 seen on a radar at Miami, Florida. The bright spiral bands represent regions of rainfall. The circular marker is at a range of 100 nautical miles (185 km). Courtesy L. F. Conover, National Hurricane Research Laboratory, Miami, Florida.*

outside the storm vortex. This accounts for the description of a hurricane as a warm core cyclone. Strongest upwards velocities are found outside the region of peak winds and are regions of convective clouds and thunderstorms. They are not symmetrically distributed around the storm. Instead there are often spiral bands of precipitation with the heaviest concentrations in the right-forward quadrant of the hurricane. This is the region where tornadoes are most likely to develop. The pattern of clouds and precipitation stands out clearly on radar scopes (Fig. 6–11) and on photographs taken from Earth orbiting satellites (Fig. 6–12).

Hurricanes develop over warm oceans and derive most of their energy from the underlying water. The precise mechanism by which they are formed still is not clear. What is known is that there are many pressure disturbances over the tropical oceans and that a small percentage become hurricanes. For example, over the Atlantic Ocean in an average year, there are about 100 rain storms detected by means of weather satellites. When the winds in these weak storms are less than 17.5 m sec^{-1} (39 mph), they are called *tropical depressions*. Some of them originate as low pressure systems which formed over the African continent and propagate westward.

In an average year, mostly during the months of September, October,

FIGURE 6–12 *Hurricane Inez photographed from ESSA Weather Satellite on October 5, 1966. This storm was just southwest of Florida whose boundaries have been drawn on the photograph. Courtesy U.S. Department of Commerce, NOAA.*

and November, some 10 depressions intensify and are given the name *tropical storms*. This means that peak winds are between 17.5 and 32.4 m sec^{-1} (39 to 73 mph). Six of these storms reach hurricane strength and two cross a United States coastline. In fact, the number of Atlantic hurricanes varies greatly from year to year, sometimes being more than ten. Since the advent of systematic satellite cloud surveillance of the earth, it has been observed that the number of tropical storms and hurricanes is greater than was once suspected.

As suggested in Fig. 6–8, the most common paths followed by hurricanes are determined by the prevailing wind patterns. The storms are transported by the easterly trade winds and then curve poleward as they approach the continents. As you might suspect, this is an oversimplification because the wind patterns sometimes differ markedly from the averages represented by the general circulation of the atmosphere. A hurricane is transported by the

Severe storms

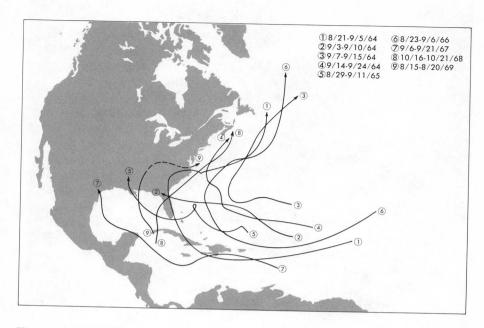

FIGURE 6–13 *The tracks of selected Atlantic hurricanes which occurred between 1964 and 1970.*

major current of air in which it is located while, at the same time, to a lesser extent, moving through the current. As the current changes, the hurricane path changes. At times this occurs suddenly and by large amounts. Figure 6–13 shows actual storm tracks of hurricanes over the western North Atlantic Ocean. It is evident that, in some cases, the storm track can change abruptly.

As hurricanes move over land or over higher latitude oceans, they become weaker. This occurs primarily because the energy input is reduced as the storm moves away from regions of warm ocean water. In addition when a hurricane passes over a continent, the terrain exerts additional frictional forces which act to reduce the wind speeds.

Hurricanes moving over land can be very destructive and lethal. A single storm, such as Hurricane Camille in August 1969, can do about one and a half billion dollars of damage. The hurricane which passed over Bangladesh in November 1970, reportedly took more than 250,000 lives. The main cause of damage and loss of life is the wave of ocean water produced by the hurricane winds as the storm approaches a coast. A "wall" of water some three meters or more in height can be produced. It can sweep over low-lying land, and coupled with torrential rains, can cause flooding on a massive scale. Evacuation to high ground is the only sure means of survival.

Severe storms

Over the open oceans, hurricane winds can produce waves of spectacular heights. They depend on the strength of the wind, the size of the storm, and its duration. In the Atlantic, an average hurricane produces waves some 10 to 12 m high. Waves generated in different quadrants of the storm cross one another, producing wave peaks which may be higher than 15 m. In extreme cases they may exceed 20 m. Such waves were reported in 1935 by a Japanese naval vessel which inadvertently sailed into a typhoon. As one can imagine, the waves can easily toss even the largest ship around and make sailing through a hurricane a terrifying experience.

The waves produced by a hurricane propagate outwards in all directions. Those initiated in the right-hand side of the storm move rapidly in the direction of the storm's movement. A typical hurricane may travel at a speed of 5 to 6 m sec^{-1} and advance about 500 km in a day. The storm-generated waves propagate much faster, covering a distance of about 1,000 to 1,500 km in a day. As the waves leave the storm region, their amplitudes diminish, the crests take on a flatter shape, and the waves are called swells. Before the days of orbiting satellites, radar, and airplanes, the arrival of swells was often the only warning to sailors and coastal dwellers that a hurricane was imminent.

In some cases, dissipating tropical storms move over land and, in the case of mountainous or hilly terrain, may yield very heavy rainfalls. In June 1972, hurricane Agnes dumped enormous quantities of rain on Virginia, Maryland, Delaware, Pennsylvania, and surrounding states. As a result there were floods of devastating proportions, with damage estimated in excess of three billion dollars.

The strong winds in a hurricane do a great deal of destruction to man-made structures and vegetation. Huge trees can be blown over and loose objects carried away. Wind damage is most severe near the coast line because the peak wind speed near the ground decreases as the storm passes over land.

Fortunately, by means of weather satellites, radar, and specially equipped airplanes, hurricanes can be detected early in their development and tracked throughout their existence. Modern forecasting and communication techniques make it possible to warn people in areas likely to be affected in sufficient time so that they can take steps needed to reduce property damage and move to high ground. More will be said about hurricanes in Chapter 8 where a discussion is given of attempts being made to weaken them by means of cloud seeding.

7

Climates of the Earth

When a meteorologist talks about the weather, he refers to short term variations of the state of the atmosphere. This would include consideration of such things as air temperature, cloudiness, precipitation, and winds as they change from minute to minute or even from one month to the next.

The long term manifestations of the weather are called the climate. Stated in another way, the climate of any region is represented by the statistical properties of the weather over an extended period, typically several decades.

It is essential, when speaking of the climate, to delineate the region involved. For example, as will be seen later in this chapter, a great deal of attention has been given to the climate of the entire Earth. But studies have also been made of the climate inside a house or over a corn field.

The word *microclimate* is often used to specify the climate structure of the atmosphere between the Earth's surface and a height where the Earth's influence becomes indistinguishable. Such a layer, measured in terms of meters or tens of meters, is of great importance in many practical problems. This is the region where people live and vegetation grows. The number of bushels of corn or wheat yielded by a field is determined to a significant extent by the microclimate of the field.

Climatologists have studied the properties of the air in confined places such as the inside of buildings. Recently, the conditions within greenhouses have been getting a great deal of attention. To an increasing extent they are being used for commercial farming. Since the interior climates can be controlled to a large extent, greenhouse farming can produce astounding quantities of produce such as tomatoes and cucumbers for each acre under cover.

The climate characteristics of regions perhaps 10 to 100 km in size can be classified as part of a *mesoclimate*. For example, the atmospheric properties of a valley or of a city fall into this category. The term *macroclimate* is used to describe conditions over large areas, perhaps covering a state, country, or even a continent. When the entire planet is considered as a whole, it is appropriate to talk about the planetary or global climate.

The grouping of climates·according to the size of the region under consideration is only one form of classification. There are many other schemes, a few of which are widely known and used, particularly by geographers and agriculturalists. As we shall see, some of them have important correlations with the characteristics of the native vegetation.

Descriptive Climatology

Most often the climate of a region is described in terms of the averages of temperature, precipitation, atmospheric humidity, and wind velocity over periods on the order of 30 to 40 years. A complete description of the climate should also include such items as the variations of these quantities throughout the year and from year to year. The importance of this idea can be illustrated by the curves in Fig. 7–1 showing the mean monthly temperatures of San Francisco, St. Louis, and Baltimore. The annual average temperatures of these cities are close to one another but the climates are different. St. Louis and Baltimore have more extreme temperatures—hotter in summer and colder in the winter than the west coast city.

Traditionally, climatology has involved the analysis of large amounts of data. Observations from stations all over the world have been accumulating for a long time. In some places, they go back some two centuries or more, while in others, the record length is measured only in decades. Although there are some island stations with long records, and in some places there have been shipboard measurements, for the most part, observations over the oceans are inadequate for the construction of their climatologies.

By taking averages of the available data and extrapolating between stations, maps have been made showing certain features of the climate. Figure

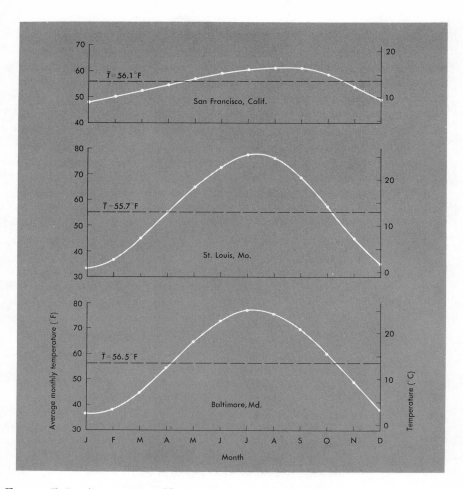

FIGURE 7–1 *Average monthly temperatures in San Francisco, St. Louis, and Baltimore. The dashed line,* T, *shows annual average temperature.*

7–2 shows average January and July surface air temperatures over the Earth. Certain features are immediately evident. In general, temperatures decrease from equator towards the poles but the changes are not regular by any means. There are pronounced differences between summer and winter. For example, in summer the oceans are cooler than the land; in winter the opposite is true. Over the land the extreme values tend to occur over the interior parts of continents. Outside Antarctica, the lowest recorded surface air temperature is the −67°C measured in Verkhoyansk, Siberia. It also has recorded summer temperatures as high as 32°C. The highest temperature ever recorded was 58°C at El Azizia in Libya.

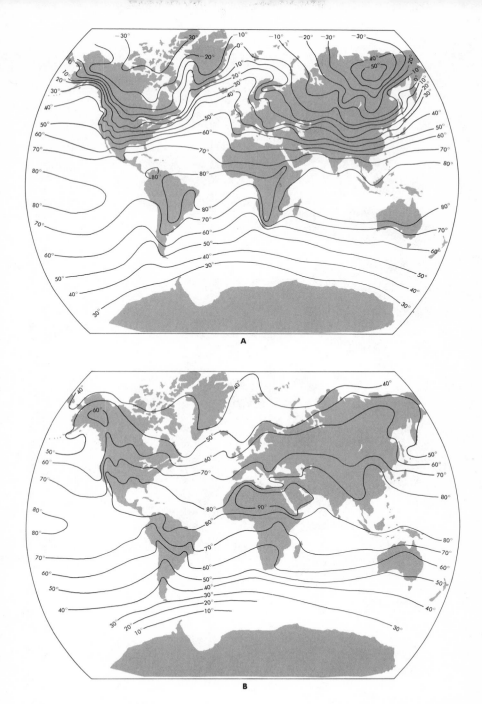

FIGURE 7–2 *Average surface temperatures in degrees Fahrenheit over the Earth in January (A) and July (B). From H. R. Byers,* General Meteorology, *McGraw Hill Book Company, 1959.*

Climates of the Earth

FIGURE 7–3 Simplified pattern of the average annual precipitation in centimeters over the Earth. Based mostly on data from B. Haurwitz and J. M. Austin, Climatology, McGraw Hill Book Company, 1944.

Climates of the Earth

The changes of air temperatures over the oceans from summer to winter are much smaller than they are over the continents. As noted earlier, there are several reasons for this result. Solar radiation penetrates more deeply into water than it does into the soil, and the mixing of ocean waters distributes the heat through a very large mass of water. Over land, heat absorbed in the surface layers is conducted downward through the soil and rocks very slowly. As a consequence, the available insolation is used to heat a relatively small mass. Also, as is shown in Table 3–1, the specific heat of water is higher than the specific heat of soil and rock. This means that a greater number of calories are required to increase the temperature of water 1°C than would be required to warm soil or rocks by the same 1°C. In winter the ocean loses heat by radiation to outer space more slowly than does the land.

The oceans represent a huge reservoir of heat. They add heat to the atmosphere during the cold season of the year and serve to take heat out of the atmosphere during the warm season.

The average annual precipitation over the Earth is shown in Fig. 7–3. As would be expected, the heaviest amounts occur over equatorial regions and over mountainous areas often invaded by tropical maritime air.

The southern slopes of the Himalaya Mountains are among the wettest on Earth. Cherrapunji in India gets an average of 11.4 m of rain, mostly during the summer monsoon in June through September. One year the depth of rainfall reached the staggering amount of 26.5 m. The station reporting the world's greatest yearly average rainfall of 11.7 m is on Mt. Waialeale in Hawaii. The precipitation is produced in clouds formed as warm, humid, tropical air ascends over the mountain slopes.

The annual distribution of precipitation may differ greatly from one region to the next. Figure 7–4 gives several examples. Most of the precipitation in San Francisco falls from cyclonic storms moving in from the Pacific during the winter. In many places, such as Cherrapunji, the major fraction of the rain falls from summer showers and thunderstorms. In some other localities, such as Tucson, Arizona, there are two rainy seasons—a summer maximum from convective storms in moist, tropical air and a winter maximum from traveling cyclones. In still others, precipitation falls throughout the year with relatively little change from season to season.

The variation of precipitation from month to month, of course, is only one important characteristic of the climate. The total annual amounts and their variabilities from year to year also are crucial factors. A desert region such as southern Arizona is characterized by low annual precipitation which, in terms of percent, varies greatly from year to year. On the other hand, places over the humid eastern part of the United States have higher precipitation which is more dependable than is the rain in the desert. As a result, dry land farming is successful in places such as Illinois and Iowa, but in Ari-

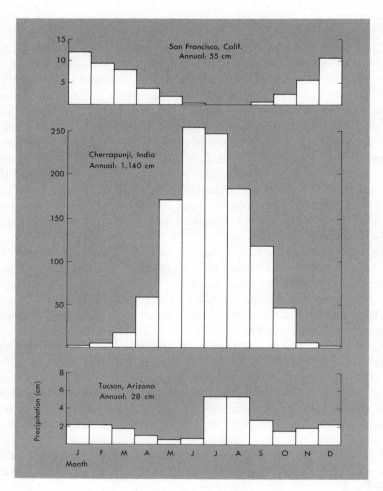

FIGURE 7–4   *Mean monthly precipitation at Tucson, Arizona and Cherrapunji, India. Note the differences in the ordinate scale.*

zona and Southern California most agriculture is impossible without irrigation.

Climate Classifications

The most widely used classication of world climates was devised in Austria by Wladimir Köppen. It was first published in 1918 and modified several times in subsequent years. It is based mostly on annual and monthly averages of temperature and precipitation. Köppen was confronted with the fact that the spacing of observing stations was inadequate to delineate climatic regions, a situation which still exists. To overcome this problem, he used the distribution of natural vegetation to indicate the boundaries of various climatic regions.

Another well-know climatic classification is named after its American originator C. Warren Thornthwaite. It also is founded on the notion that natural vegetation is an indicator of climate, and it classifies climates on that basis. Of particular importance in Thornthwaite's scheme is the difference between the mean monthly distribution of precipitation and a quantity called *evapotranspiration*. It is the quantity of moisture lost through evaporation from the soil and through transpiration from the vegetation.

Various climatologists, among them H. Flohn in Germany, have proposed that purely descriptive classifications such as those of Köppen and Thornthwaite are inadequate. Flohn argued that a satisfactory classification should take into account the causes for the climate. In 1950, he proposed a scheme which takes the general circulation of the atmosphere as one of the starting points in explaining the climatic patterns over the Earth. This concept has received a great deal of attention and support in recent years. A better understanding of the physical factors controlling the climate are needed in order to explain why the climate of the Earth has changed in the past and what it is likely to do in the future. More will be said about these points in a later section of this chapter.

It has long been known that certain aspects of the climate depend on the latitude, the altitude of the place, and its location with respect to large water and land masses. As would be expected, the greater the elevation and the more poleward the station, the lower the average temperature is likely to be. Also since the temperatures of oceans and large lakes change much less than do the temperatures of the continents, places just downwind from such bodies of water are not likely to experience the extremes of hot and cold as are locations far downwind. For example, cities along the west coast of the United States have smaller ranges of temperature than those in the central and eastern part of the country. The term *maritime climate* is sometimes used when referring to conditions at localities greatly influenced by the sea—at San Francisco for example.

Places over large land masses are said to experience *continental climates*, and they typically exhibit relatively large temperature ranges from summer to winter.

The variations of temperature through the day are also greater over continents than along windward coastal areas in general. The diurnal temperature range is greatest at low latitude stations where the atmosphere is dry. For example, desert areas in the tropics sometimes have diurnal temperature ranges exceeding 20°C. There is efficient solar heating during the day, and rapid cooling during the night as infrared radiation is lost to outer space.

In Chapter 3, a discussion was given of the general circulation of the atmosphere. An examination of the air motions and the regions of high and low pressure explains many aspects of the distribution of climates around the world. As was noted earlier, in the high-pressure areas there is generally subsiding air motion. It acts to raise the air temperature as it sinks. This reduces the relative humidity and inhibits the growth of clouds and precipitation. The result is that under the semipermanent anticyclones there are deserts particularly on the eastern sides where the sinking is most pronounced.

The rainfall map in Fig. 7–3 shows that extensive deserts exist over the western parts of the continents and other regions where anticyclonic motion predominates. Examples are the Sonoran Desert in the southewestern United States and Mexico, the extensive desert along the west coast of South America and North Africa. It is important to recognize that the areas of deficient rainfall extend over the adjacent oceans. This should be recalled when it is proposed that the construction of an artificial lake will increase rainfall in a desert region. In nature a scarcity of rainfall generally can be attributed to the subsidence of air which inhibits the growth of rain clouds rather than the absence of a nearby source of water vapor.

On the other hand, wet climates are found in regions with strong, persistent ascending air motions, particularly if the air is warm and humid. These conditions are commonly found along the intertropical convergence zone. Mountain ranges force air upwards as well as acting as sources for convective clouds when their slopes are warm. As a result, precipitation over mountainous areas generally are higher than over flat lands. When the air moving up the mountain slopes is both humid and unstable, spectacular amounts of rain can fall. We have already cited some examples.

Figure 7–3 illustrates how the Rocky Mountains along the west coast of the United States and Canada experience heavy precipitation on their windward sides. The prevailing winds are westerly and they carry moist air from over the Pacific Ocean. Note however that on the leeward side of the front range of mountains, desert conditions are found. For example, in eastern Washington, precipitation is less than 25 cm per year. This is known as a *rain shadow.*

As the air in the westerlies moves up the western slopes of the mountains, its relative humidity increases. Clouds develop and rain and snow fall to the ground. When the air then passes over the mountains and sinks into the lower elevations it warms adiabatically. Since water substance has been removed, the descending air is left much drier than when it passed over the coast line. Clouds and precipitation do not occur readily in the subsiding air, and the result is a desert.

The seasonal climates of an area are indicated by the general circulation. As shown in Fig. 3–3, the air currents in the middle of the atmosphere meander around the Earth in a series of troughs and ridges. On the average, regions with winds from a northerly direction are colder than those where the winds have a southerly component. There also tends to be more precipitation over regions under pressure troughs. As a result, the eastern parts of the United States are cold and wet in an average winter.

In certain years, for reasons which still are not known, the pattern of troughs and ridges in the pressure field are shifted drastically from their average positions. For example, a deep 500-mb trough may become established over the western part of the United States. In such a circumstance, the western states may have abnormally wet, cold weather. At the same time the eastern states would be abnormally warm and dry.

Sometimes the entire pattern of pressure troughs and ridges over the Northern Hemisphere shifts longitudinally. When this happens weather abnormalities occur in a great many places. For example, if it is unusually warm and dry in New England, it should not be surprising to learn that western Europe is abnormally cold or that parts of the Soviet Union are abnormally warm and dry.

In summary, the flow patterns in the general circulation of the atmosphere exert major controls over the climate. In addition, the topography and the proximity of large bodies of water can have important influences. Prolonged deviations of the pattern of air motions from those observed in the average pattern of the general circulation lead to unusual seasonal or annual weather. In some circumstances, the consequences can be droughts or at the other extreme, floods.

Climate of the Earth

A subject of increasing interest these days is the climate of the entire Earth, how it has changed over time and whether human activity is influencing it.

We have known for a long time that far into the distant past there were slow but very major changes in climate. They appear in geological records as ice ages, interspersed with long lasting warm intervals. Table 7–1 shows periods of known glaciations over the last 600 million years. During the ice ages, large regions of the Earth were covered with sheets of ice which advanced equatorward, in extreme cases reaching to latitudes of 40° over the continents.

As might be expected, the more recent past has received the most attention of geophysicists. The Pleistocene Epoch covering the last 600,000 years has been studied extensively by paleoclimatologists who have used a variety of techniques for dating relics and for estimating the temperatures during

Table 7-1

Geologic Eras, Periods, and Epochs of Known Major Glaciations

Era	Period	Epoch	Beginning of Interval (Millions of Years Ago)
Paleozoic	Cambrian	....	600
	Ordovician	....	500
	Silurian	....	430
	Devonian	....	400
	Carboniferous {	Mississippian	350
		Pennsylvanian	330
	Permian	....	275
Mesozoic	Triassic	....	225
	Jurassic	....	180
	Cretaceous	....	135
Cenozoic	Tertiary	Paleocene	66
		Eocene	59
		Oligocene	38
		Miocene	25
		Pliocene	12
	Quaternary	Pleistocene	0.6
		Holocene	0.01

Source: W. .D. Sellers, *Physical Climatology*, University of Chicago Press, 1965.

their formation.* Unfortunately a completely reliable method for dating events between 150,000 and 10,000,000 years old does not exist. This fact coupled with contradictory findings in various parts of the world has prevented the construction of a consistent geological calendar over the Pleistocene or even a major fraction of it. Nevertheless, the available evidence does allow some estimates of the major climatic occurrences.

The Pleistocene Epoch experienced at least four major glacial ages during which the average temperature of the Earth was about 6°C below today's average value. Each ice age lasted about one hundred thousand years, except for the last one called the Wisconsin Age which extended from about 40,000 to 10,000 years ago. The interglacial ages were warm periods with temperatures of the Earth averaging about 3° higher than those of today.

*For a discussion of geological dating techniques, see D. L. Eicher, *Geologic Time*, Prentice-Hall, 1968.

Table 7–2

A Brief Chronology of the Climate of the Last 10,000 Years

Dates	Region	Climate
9000–6000 B.C.	Southern Arizona	Warm and arid
7800–6800 B.C.	Europe	Cool and moist, becoming cool and dry by 7000 B.C.
6800–5600 B.C.	North America, Europe	Cool and dry, with possible extinction of mammals, particularly in Arizona and New Mexico
5600–2500 B.C.	Both hemispheres	Warm and moist, becoming warm and dry by 3000 B.C. (Climatic Optimum)
2500–500 B.C.	Northern hemisphere	Generally warm and dry with periods of heavy rain and intense droughts
500 B.C.–A.D. 0	Europe	Cool and moist; glacial maximum in Scandinavia and Ireland between 500 and 200 B.C.
330	United States	Drought in the Southwest
600	Alaska	Glacial advance
590–645	Near East, England	Severe drought in the Near East, followed by cold winters; drought in England
673	Near East	Black Sea frozen
800	Mexico	Start of moist period
800–801	Near East	Black Sea frozen
829	Africa	Ice on the Nile
900–1200	Iceland	Glacial recession (Viking period)
1000–1011	Africa	Ice on the Nile
1000–1100	Utah	Snowline 300 m higher than today
1200	Alaska	Glacial advance
1180–1215	United States	Wet in the West
1220–1290	United States	Drought in the West
1276–1299	United States	"Great Drought" in the Southwest
1300–1330	United States	Wet in the West
1500–1900	Europe, United States	Generally cool and dry; periodic glacial advances in Europe (1541 to 1680, 1741 to 1770, and 1801 to 1890) and North America (1700 to 1750); drought in the southwestern United States from 1573 to 1593
1880–1940	Both hemispheres	Increase of winter temperature by 1.5°C; drop of 5.2 m in the level of the Great Salt Lake; Alpine glaciation reduced by 25 percent and Arctic ice by 40 percent; rapid glacial recession in the Patagonian Andes (1910–1920) and the Canadian Rockies (1931–1938)
1942–1960	Both hemispheres	Worldwide temperature decrease and halt of glacial recession

Source: W. D. Sellers, *Physical Climatology*, University of Chicago Press, 1965.

Looking more closely at the recent records, researchers have found that during the Wisconsin Age starting about 40,000 years ago, there have been four glacial advances. One of the best documented, which started some 23,000 years ago, was accompanied by temperatures over the Central Atlantic Ocean, the Caribbean, and Europe which were about 10°C colder that present temperatures. The climate of the United States was wet and cool with glaciation over the central part of the country extending as far south as Iowa and Nebraska.

Data on the climate over the last 10,000 years has been fairly extensive. Table 7–2 contains a small sampling of certain important features of the climate. Of particular note is the interval 5600 to 2500 B.C. when the atmosphere was 2 to 3° warmer than it is now and conditions were moist, particularly over North Africa and the Middle East. It is known as a Climatic Optimum because conditions were favorable for development of plants and animals.

The most recent cold period, known as the Little Ice Age, occurred fairly recently, from 1500 to 1900 A.D. During these four hundred years, it was generally cool and dry and there were equatorward advances of glaciers and sea ice.

At the start of this century a pronounced warming began over the earth

FIGURE 7–5 *Change of mean annual temperatures for various latitude bands during the period 1870 to 1967 according to analyses of J. Murray Mitchell. Reprinted from* Man's Impact on the Climate *edited by William H. Matthews, et al. by permission of The M.I.T. Press, Cambridge, Massachusetts, 1971.*

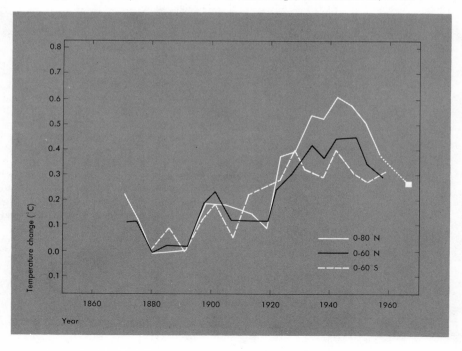

as a whole. Data are sufficiently numerous to construct the curve shown in Fig. 7–5. Over about half a century, temperatures increased about 0.6°C. The warming was accompanied by a poleward displacement of the edges of sea ice, a melting and retreat of glaciers and a small increase in sea level. As shown in Fig. 5–12, in extreme cases of glacier growth or shrinkage, sea level could change by many tens of meters. Imagine the devastation of the coastal cities of the world if sea level were to rise a few meters.

Since about 1940, there has been a gradual cooling of the atmosphere which has continued into the 1970's. Sea ice has been thickening and advancing equatorward. At least for the present, glaciers have begun to grow, and the threat of rising ocean waters can be put aside. Instead, certain scientists with a gloomy outlook have raised the possibility that we are headed for another ice age.

Hypotheses on Climatic Change

It is now recognized that a single hypothesis can not account for the observed climatic changes over the entire history of the Earth. The problem of explaining ancient climates is a formidable one because it must include the changing configuration of continents and oceans.* There is little doubt that the ice ages some 100 to 400 million years ago can be attributed to a large extent, to alterations in the pattern of land and sea as the continental masses drifted with respect to one another.

Many scientists are interested in learning to what extent the climate variations over the more recent past can be explained in terms of the behavior of the atmosphere and oceans on a global scale. We know that the climate is related to the strength and character of the general circulation, but it still is not clear which factor or factors govern the variations in the general circulation.

Many hypotheses have been offered. They may be divided into two classes: (1) those assuming that there have been changes in the amount of energy reaching the Earth, primarily from the Sun; (2) those assuming that incoming solar radiation is constant and that climate changes are caused by modification in the properties of the Earth's surface or of the atmosphere.

Various climatologists have related certain characteristics of the general circulation and climate to sunspot number. One of the best known theories was proposed in 1953 by Hurd Willett, then at the Massachusetts Institute of Technology. He suggested that the modulations in climate were not caused by gradual variations in solar radiation, but rather by the more irregular ones associated with solar eruptions. He compared fluctuations in

*See S. P. Clark, Jr., *Structure of the Earth*, Prentice-Hall, 1971.

climate over a 200-year period with the frequency of sunspots observed over the same interval. On the basis of this admittedly short record, Willett suggested that there is an 80-year cycle in the climate associated with a similar cycle in sunspot occurrence.

Although Willett's ideas are not widely accepted, they received some support from analyses which revealed that increased solar activity was followed, some days later, by shifts in the general circulation of the atmosphere.

The state of uncertainty in explaining changes in climate can be illustrated by citing some of the theories which have been advanced by established scientists. It has been proposed that volcanism might account for the formation of ice ages in the following way. Volcanic eruptions introduce massive quantities of dust into the atmosphere (see Fig. 1–2), and it has been argued that the dust would reduce the amount of absorbed solar energy and lead to lower temperatures. Recent work shows this hypothesis has serious shortcomings. Whether particles in the atmosphere cause net warming or cooling depends on the characteristics of the particles, the altitudes at which they exist, and the reflectivity of the underlying surface.

Some authors have proposed that changes in climate have been caused by variations in the carbon dioxide concentration in the atmosphere. Volcanic eruptions were the major sources of CO_2 before the combustion of fossil fuels became widespread. Yet most scientists believe that unrealistically large changes in the concentration of CO_2 would have been needed to explain temperature changes known to have occurred over geological time.

Still another hypothesis for explaining the ice ages proposes that there have been changes of the Earth's orbit around the Sun.

Unfortunately, as noted by William D. Sellers[*], at the University of Arizona, "at the present time, a critical evaluation of the many theories of climatic change that have been presented is hampered by our lack of knowledge of the physical environment in which we live."

Recently geophysicists have focused a great deal of attention on the variations of the earth's temperature over the last century (Fig. 7–5). They have been particularly interested in learning if the warming and cooling could be attributed to human activity.

There is no doubt that man has changed the environment in many ways. As noted in Chapter 1, the composition of the atmosphere has been altered somewhat. There has been a significant increase in the concentration of carbon dioxide, and to a lesser extent, increases in the concentrations of other gases and particulates. Oil spillage from ships and drilling operations have produced a film of oil over most of the ocean surface. Forests and

[*]W.D. Sellers, Physical Climatology, University of Chicago Press, 1965.

fields have been cleared and replaced by highways and cities. Large quantities of heat are put into the atmosphere, rivers, and lakes.

Not too many years ago, the increases in temperature during the first half of this century were attributed, at least tentatively, by various authors to the increase of carbon dioxide which occurred over the same period. It was argued that the carbon dioxide would absorb some of the terrestrial infrared radiation which would normally escape to outer space through the "windows" in the water vapor absorption spectrum. There still are debates over how much additional absorption actually would occur for a given increase in CO_2 concentration. Notwithstanding the uncertainties, when the worldwide increases in atmospheric CO_2 were accompanied by increases in temperature, there was some concern about the future climate.

As noted in Chapter 1, the rise of CO_2 concentration in the atmosphere over the last 70 years can be ascribed to the burning of fossil fuels. Roughly half of the released CO_2 is retained in the atmosphere while the remainder is absorbed by the oceans or taken up by plants. It has been estimated that by the end of the twentieth century, the CO_2 concentration will be about 380 ppm. If no other factors were operating, the continual increase of CO_2 in the atmosphere could lead to continual warming. *But this increase does not act alone.* Since the middle forties, worldwide temperatures have been decreasing (Fig. 7–5) even though CO_2 is still increasing.

A number of scientists have speculated that the cooling in recent decades may be attributable to an increase of particulates in the atmosphere. A careful analysis of the problem shows that if all other factors were constant and the aerosol content of the atmosphere was increased, air temperatures near the ground would not necessarily decrease. As noted earlier, the result would depend on the altitudes at which the particles occurred as well as their properties and the reflectivity of the Earth.

The available observations of atmospheric particles paint a confusing picture of the trends over the planet as a whole. The curves shown in Chapter 1 (Fig. 1–2) indicate that over Mauna Loa, Hawaii, the values of turbidity in 1971 were at about the same level as they were in the late fifties and early sixties. It is evident that substantial increases in atmospheric particulates following large volcanic eruptions were removed from the atmosphere after a period of several years.

Measurements over the North Atlantic Ocean indicate that the particle concentration nearly doubled between 1907 and 1970. The same observational technique showed no change in particulate loading over the South Pacific.

In summary, the limited data which exist do not readily support the notion that atmospheric cooling since the forties can be simply attributed to increased particulate pollution.

Theoretical studies of the general circulation make it abundantly clear that climate variations can not be explained by examining one or two of the variable properties of the atmosphere or the surface below it. As was mentioned earlier, the general circulation is a complex mechanism with many feedbacks and *second-order effects*. A change in one feature causes changes in others which react with the first, and so forth. For example, an increase in temperature may cause an increase in evaporation, a rise in relative humidity, and atmospheric instability. The result could be the formation of clouds which are better reflectors than the Earth's surface, a decrease in the amount of solar radiation reaching the lower atmosphere, and a cooling of the lower atmosphere.

Many atmospheric scientists have expressed the view that adequate explanation of climatic fluctuations and of possible human influences requires the development of much better theoretical models than exist today. It is hoped that an adequate mathematical model can be developed which takes into account the many interacting factors in a realistic way.

The observations already in the meteorological archives around the world are of much value in describing how the climate has varied over the last few centuries, but they are far from adequate. They do not include measurements of the chemical compositions of the air.

It is essential that there be more adequate, systematic measurements of the properties of the atmosphere and of the surface characteristics of the continents and oceans Such data will serve as a history of climatic changes over the years and will hopefully lead to an adequate explanation of the climate of the Earth.

8

Applications

The weather and climate affect people and their possessions in a great many ways; some are obvious, but others are so subtle that they may not be recognized. For example, there is considerable evidence that the weather can have important physical and psychological influences on some individuals. Many have reported correlations between asthmatic, arthritic, or sinus troubles and some aspects of the weather. These claims have some validity even though they cannot be explained adequately.

When a strong foehn wind is blowing (Chapter 2), many people experience distinct psychological as well as physical reactions. The latter are attributable to the high temperature and extreme dryness. It is not clear why the winds are accompanied by increases in instability, headaches, and suicides.

Various authors have related the decisions of great men such as Abraham Lincoln to the state of the atmosphere. Of course, when you set out to find relationships you often succeed even if real ones do not exist. Nevertheless, it is certainly true that sometimes the weather makes you feel good while on other occasions it has the opposite effect. A warm, sunny day after a long, cold winter makes the world seem brighter.

There are many direct ways by which the weather affects life on Earth. In earlier chapters the disastrous effects of violent storms were mentioned. The importance of adequate quantities of rain and snow are obvious.

We can be sure that over the ages, man has sought to learn the nature of the atmosphere and use that information to improve his circumstances. As better techniques for observations and communications have developed and as science and technology have advanced, we have been using the accumulating knowledge to ever-increasing degrees.

Use of Climatological Data

Available climatological data has a great many applications. For example, when building airports it is essential that the runways be aligned along the direction of the prevailing winds because airplanes take off and land into the wind. A diagram such as the one shown in Fig. 8–1, assembled from past observations, and called a "wind rose," shows that the surface wind is most often from the southeast in this particular area and tells an airport designer the direction he should use when laying out the runways.

Successful farming depends on the intelligent use of climatological information. The planting of crops must take into account the dates when temperatures are likely to fall below the freezing point as well as the length and characteristics of the growing season. Frost-sensitive vegetables cannot be put into the fields until the likelihood of a killing frost is quite small. At the same time, plant scientists can specify the number of days of above-freezing temperatures needed for most crops and therefore put limits on

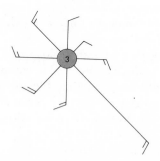

FIGURE 8–1   A wind rose for Tucson, Arizona showing the relative frequency of various wind directions. The length of the arrow is proportional to the percent of occasions with wind from that direction. The number in the center gives the percent of observations with calm winds. The average wind speed in knots is shown by the barbs. Each full length barb equals 5 knots.

the kind of vegetation which can be expected to thrive in any climatological regime.

A knowledge of the climate is also important to ranchers, dairymen, and chicken growers. Certain animals react in a very distinct way to the temperature and humidity conditions. When it is too hot and humid, the production of domestic animals decreases. They eat less and produce fewer eggs or less milk; cattle and hogs increase in weight slowly. A modern farmer uses a knowledge of the climate to plan shelters for his livestock during the period of the year when it is expected to be excessively hot or cold.

The airline industry must be well informed on the climate and weather. This was recognized in the early days of aviation and accounts for the fact that airline companies played important roles in the establishment of weather observing stations all over the globe. It is necessary to know the prevailing wind direction for runway alignment, as we noted already, and for efficient airplane operation much more meteorological information is needed.

The length of runways required for the takeoff of an airplane depends on the properties of the air near the ground. As the air gets warmer and more humid, its density decreases. The density also decreases with increasing altitude. Whatever the reason, the lower the density, the greater must be the airplane speed in order for the aerodynamic lift forces to be sufficient for the airplane to take off and climb. For this reason, in places such as Tucson, Arizona, where it is not unusual to experience temperatures above 40°C (100°F) on summer afternoons, long takeoff runs are required when a large, heavily loaded airplane leaves the field. The same is true at Denver which is at an elevation of about 1,600 m above sea level. At such high places, the takeoffs are even longer when high temperatures and humidities occur.

The reader can certainly think of many other ways in which a knowledge of the average state of the atmosphere can be used beneficially. One place where it has not been used adequately is in city planning. For example, would it not be reasonable to have industrial sites and other producers of air pollutants downwind of residential areas? Unfortunately, in many places the zoning boards do not take the climatological characteristics of the region into account.

Weather Forecasting

Climatological data are widely used and of substantial value in planning a wide variety of human endeavors. In many circumstances, accurate predictions of the weather can be of even greater value.

Applications

For certain purposes, a correct forecast even a few minutes in advance would be very worthwhile. For example, knowledge that a tornado will strike a building, say a school, in five minutes would permit the occupants to take protective action. At busy airports, such as O'Hare in Chicago, a precise prediction that a fog will close the airport in five minutes would be of great help to the airplane controllers as well as to the pilots. At O'Hare, airplanes sometimes land and take off more frequently than one per minute. If, at the last minute before landing, airplanes have to be flagged off and sent to other localities, even minutes can mean great savings in cost as well as safe operations.

Most weather forecasts are made from several hours to perhaps two days in advance. Predictions of daily rainfall and temperature are made regularly up to periods of three and five days. For longer stretches of time up to perhaps a month, general outlooks of average temperatures can be made, but the longer the period, the less accurate the forecast.

When measuring the skill of a forecaster, it is not enough to ask the percentage of accurate forecasts. This point can be illustrated by examining how well we can forecast rain in Yuma, Arizona during the very dry months of May and June. Over the period 1960 to 1969, measurable rain (greater than 0.25 mm) fell on only four out of a total of 610 days. Therefore, the chance of rain was less than one percent. It is likely to remain close to that in the future. Anyone knowing these facts can predict "no rain" for Yuma for every day of May and June, 1990 with confidence of being right close to 99 percent of the time. The percentage is high but it is not a measure of forecasting skill; it is an indication that there is predictive value in climatological data. As already noted, such information is very worthwhile, but to demonstrate skill a weather forecaster should be able to do better than merely using climatology. It can lead to a high fraction of correct specifications of the weather but miss the changes in weather. In Yuma, for example, a good forecast would accurately predict those rare days on which rain does occur.

Meteorologists have devised many schemes for evaluating their skill. The better ones are those which compare their forecasts with the actual climatological expectations.

The procedure used by weather forecasters is to examine the latest observations of the weather and the state of the atmosphere and then predict the changes expected to occur. As would be expected, the longer the forecast period, the greater the amount of information needed at the outset. This point is illustrated in Fig. 8–2. When forecasting conditions 12 to 36 hours in the future, the inertia of the atmosphere is sufficiently large so that it is enough to consider only conditions over a small part of the Earth. When the forecast period is three to five days long, it is necessary to know initial conditions over a hemisphere and take into account exchanges of energy

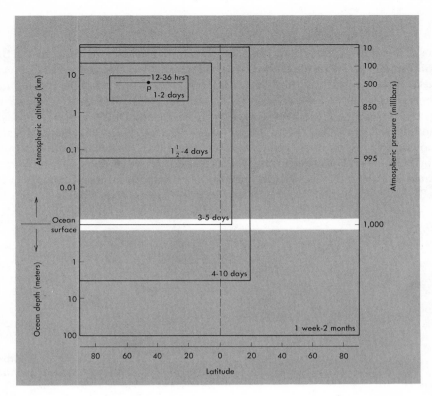

FIGURE 8–2 *Initial data over the indicated regions are required in order to pre-dict conditions at point* p *for the indicated periods. White area is the ocean-atmosphere interface zone. From J. Smagorinsky,* Bulletin of American Meteorological Society, *1967,* **48**: *89–93.*

and water vapor between the atmosphere and the Earth's surface, particularly over the oceans. If a forecast is extended to two weeks, initial conditions must be known over the entire Earth and to a depth of several meters in the oceans.

Until fairly recently, weather forecasters depended largely on subjective analyses of surface and 500-mb weather charts. By means of extrapolations and empirical rules, the location of fronts and the positions and intensities of low- and high-pressure systems were predicted. Once this was done, the actual weather (that is, clouds, precipitation, and temperatures), was estimated mostly on the basis of the airmass characteristics, wind patterns, and frontal locations. Some people, employing such techniques, produced forecasts of amazing accuracy. Unfortunately, this approach was as much an intuitive art as a science. Outstanding forecasters did not seem to be able to teach others how to do it.

Since the late forties, there has been a steady growth of the use of mathematical models for weather prediction. These procedures have been made possible by the advances in the formulation of mathematical models of the atmosphere and the development of high speed computers. The general procedure is similar to the one used to develop a theoretical model of the general circulation (see Chapter 3). A series of equations is derived to specify changes of the atmosphere with time. They take into account air motions, temperatures, humidities, evaporation at the ground, clouds, rain, snow, and various momentum, moisture, and energy transfer mechanisms. For daily weather forecasting, the National Weather Service employs a numerical model in which the atmosphere is divided into six layers (Fig. 8–3). In experimental programs on the use of numerical models to predict

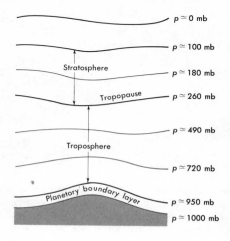

FIGURE 8–3 *The six layers of the atmosphere used by the National Weather Service in a baroclinic numerical weather prediction model. From F. G. Shuman and J. B. Hovermale,* Journal of Applied Meteorology, *1968, 7: 525–547.*

the state of the atmosphere, one to two weeks in advance, the atmosphere has been divided into as many as eleven layers.

Since the mathematical model calculates changes of the atmosphere with time, it is necessary to start with a reasonably complete and accurate knowledge of the atmosphere. Observations of the properties of the atmosphere near the Earth's surface and at the levels of interest are made twice a day at 0000 GMT and 1200 GMT by means of radiosonde stations over most of the continental areas of the Earth and from some islands and ships at sea.

At the National Meteorological Center, the process of weather analysis and prognosis is done almost entirely by computers. Observations of temperature, humidity, pressure, and wind velocity are collected; then automated techniques are used to draw maps showing the patterns of these quantities. The computers use the mathematical model to calculate pressure, temperature, and wind distributions at various levels in the atmosphere. Prognostic maps are automatically drawn for various periods up to 48 hours in the future (Fig. 8–4). In Fig. 4–5 we presented an example of an

FIGURE 8–4 Contours of atmospheric pressure or height 48 hours after the initial times: (A) 500-mb observed; (B) 500-mb predicted; (C) sea level observed; (D) sea level predicted. From F. G. Shuman and J. B. Hovermale, Journal of Applied Meteorology, 1968, 7: 525–547.

Applications

123

operational forecast made by means of a mathematical model. By predicting such quantities as vertical air motion, atmospheric stability, and humidity, the numerical models also yield patterns of expected precipitation (Fig. 8–5).

The maps of expected flow patterns and weather are transmitted all over the United States and abroad by means of a facsimile network.

The mathematical models in use in the early 1970's still do not include enough details (e.g., the effects of local terrain) to yield sufficiently accurate temperature and precipitation forecasts. For this reason, the flow patterns, cloud and precipitation configurations produced by the numerical calculations are employed as guides by weather forecasters at individual stations. To an increasing extent, the information on the prognostic charts are used as input data in statistical techniques where the weather in a particular locality is related to the values of pressure, temperature, and humidity at one or more places. Such statistical techniques lend themselves to prediction of the probable occurrence of certain weather events.

For many years, the National Weather Service used phrases such as "scattered showers" or "widespread rain" when issuing its daily forecasts. But starting about 1965, a more quantitative procedure was adopted, and precipitation forecasts have been expressed in terms of probability. For example, a forecast might read "The probability of rain today is 30 percent." It means that the chances are 3 in 10 that any random point in the forecast area will experience 0.25 mm or more of rain during the day (0800 to 2000 local time).

FIGURE 8–5   *Accumulated precipitation 12 to 24 hours after initial time: (A) observed; (B) predicted. From F. G. Shuman and J. B. Hovermale, Journal of Applied Meteorology, 1968, 7: 525–547.*

12 HOUR ACCUMULATED PRECIPITATION IN MILLIMETERS

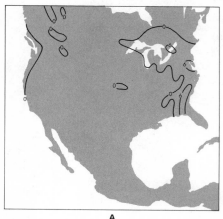
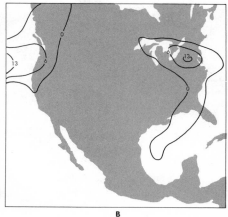

A   B

Probability forecasts take into account the nature of the precipitation as well as the confidence of the forecaster. In summer, when showers are the usual form of precipitation, low probabilities are common even when the forecaster is fairly sure some showers will occur. In the winter, widespread rain or snow are the rule, and higher precipitation probabilities are not unusual.

Since a rainfall probability forecast is a numerical measure of the likelihood that any locality will be rained on, you can guide your activities in a more rational way than if a less quantitative procedure were used. For example, if you were going on a picnic, a rainfall probability of 30 percent or less would not cause you to change your mind and stay home. On the other hand, if you were planning an activity for which rain would be ruinous, you would want a day when rainfall probability was very low—perhaps less than 5 percent. In many occupations, it is possible to calculate the losses and gains attributable to various weather phenomena. For example, an electrical utility knows the losses which are incurred when lightning causes power outages, and a construction company can calculate the losses resulting when rain prohibits the pouring of concrete. It can be shown that if reliable probability forecasts are used on a regular basis, many weather-related losses can be reduced.

Weather Modification

Although history is rich with examples of how man has tried to change the weather, significant progress dates only as far back as about 1946. That was when Vincent J. Schaefer, at General Electric's Research Laboratory, showed that Dry Ice could be used to produce ice crystals in supercooled clouds. Shortly thereafter, his colleague Bernard Vonnegut discovered that cetrain other substances, such as silver iodide and lead iodide, were effective ice nuclei (Chapter 5). They produce ice crystals when cloud temperatures are above about $-6°C$ (Table 5-1).

When a supercooled layer of stratus clouds or fog is seeded either with small particles of Dry Ice or a smoke composed of silver iodide, huge numbers of ice crystals are produced. They grow rapidly by the ice-crystal process noted in Chapter 5 and in a matter of 5 to 10 minutes fall out of the cloud leaving an opening through which the ground can be seen (Fig. 8–6). This scheme is used to clear supercooled fogs occurring over certain airports in the United States, the Soviet Union, and France.

The records reveal, however, that about 95 percent of the fogs occurring in the United States are "warm," that is, they have temperatures above $0°C$. In these cases, ice-nuclei seeding has no effect. Some warm fogs can be dissipated by seeding them with large salt particles, but this scheme is not

10:37 LST—16,100'

11:12 LST—14,250'
26 Min. After Seeding

11:20 LST—16,100'
34 Min. After Seeding

11:31 LST—16,200'
45 Min. After Seeding

FIGURE 8–6   *When this supercooled altostratus cloud was seeded with Dry Ice, a hole was produced as ice crystals grew and fell from the cloud. Courtesy Lt. Col. J. F. Church, U.S. Air Force Cambridge Research Labs.*

considered economically feasible. Fogs can be evaporated by heating them with oil burners as was done in England during World War II, but that technique is smoky and expensive. The hot blasts from jet engines lined up along a runway can dissipate fog, but they also produce turbulence which endangers small airplanes. In summary, in the mid-seventies a satisfactory procedure for clearing warm fogs from airports still did not exist.

Most efforts to change the weather have been directed towards learning how to increase rain or snowfall. The growing demands for fresh water and periodic droughts, particularly in the farming areas of the world have made the search for new sources of water a vital one.

There still is a great deal of debate among meteorolgists and statisticians about the possibility of "rainmaking" by means of cloud seeding. The chief reason for the disagreements lies with the difficulty in evaluating the results of cloud seeding experiments. For example, after a cloud or a storm system is seeded and the precipitation is measured, there is no way to determine exactly how much would have fallen if there had been *no seeding*. Weather forecasting techniques still cannot make predictions with sufficient accuracy to answer this question. The effects of seeding are expected to be relatively small in relation to the highly variable nature of precipitation. For this reason, sensitive, well-designed statistical tests must be employed. The most satisfactory approach incorporates a randomization procedure whereby only a fraction (usually about a half) of the suitable clouds or storms are seeded. Then the seeded sample is rigorously compared with the non-seeded one, and calculations are made of the likelihood that observed differences were caused by chance rather than by the seeding.

The scientific consensus in the middle 1970's was that, in certain meteorological circumstances, ice-nuclei seeding could increase precipitation by perhaps 10 to 30 percent over an area some tens of kilometers in diameter. In other circumstances seeding might decrease precipitation by the same amounts. Under still other conditions, seeding would have no effect at all. Unfortunately, little progress has been made in identifying the specific circumstances in terms of expected effects.

Still unresolved is the important question of how far downwind from the "target area" seeding effects are likely to occur. There is some evidence that they may extend more than 200 km downwind of the seeded area, but the arguments for either large-scale increases or decreases of precipitation are not conclusive and need further investigation.

Because of the destructive effects of hail, particularly to vegetation, there have been programs in many countries to develop procedures for reducing the fall of damaging hail. There is a long history of such activity. As long ago as the sixteenth century, people were ringing church bells and firing artillery to ward off severe thunderstorms. In 1750 the Archduchess of Austria prohibited the use of guns for hail suppression because of disputes between neighboring landowners over the effects of the firing. Since that time there have been various lengthy episodes in which explosives have been used in attempts to reduce hail damage. After World War II farmers in northern Italy began using rockets to carry explosives into thunderstorms threatening to hail on their fruit orchards. It is doubtful that any of these schemes had much effect on the hail.

The more scientifically founded attacks on hailstorms have sought to influence the growth of hailstones by reducing the mass of each stone and in-increasing the number of stones. In most of these efforts, it is assumed that the available supply of supercooled water in a hailstorm is essentially fixed. It is reasoned that if the number of hailstones could be increased, their average size would be reduced. It is also assumed that the number of hailstones can be increased by introducing a large number of ice nuclei into the supercooled part of the cloud. The aim is to produce hailstones small enough (less than about 5 mm) so that they will melt as they fall through the warm atmosphere below the level of the $0°C$ isotherm. In such an event, the precipitation would reach the ground as beneficial rain instead of damaging hail.

Applications

Most hailstorm seeding in the United States, Africa, Europe, and Argentina has been carried out from the ground or from airplanes. The results have been mixed and are difficult to interpret. In the Soviet Union, ice nuclei have been fired into the supercooled parts of potential hailstorms by means of artillery and rockets. Soviet scientists have reported surprisingly consistent and striking success for more than a decade. Year after year, they have claimed crop damage reduction of 60 to 80 percent. An independent test of the Soviet technique was started in the United States in 1972.

Cloud-to-ground lightning is also a serious natural hazard. It kills more people per year than do tornadoes. The fatalities usually occur one or two at a time, and therefore they do not get the attention accorded a disaster which causes widespread damage, injuries, and deaths. Everyone is familiar with the effects of lightning-caused forest and grassland fires. Some 9,000 such fires are ignited every summer in the United States.

Since about the late 1950's there have been a number of programs aimed at finding ways to reduce the occurrence of lightning. Scientists of the U.S. Forest Service have conducted experiments in which potential lightning storms have been seeded with silver iodide nuclei. It was hoped that by changing the nature of the cloud and precipitation particles, the rate of cloud charging and hence the discharge of lightning to the ground could be reduced. The research produced some encouraging results, but it still has not been shown convincingly that ice-nuclei seeding can reliably reduce the occurrence of the kind of lightning which touches off fires.

Various other schemes for influencing lightning occurrence are being tested in the United States. For example, one of them involves the introduction of millions of short metal needles into a developing cumulonimbus cloud. They are intended to prevent the build-up of electric charge centers required for the occurrence of lightning.

For reasons noted in Chapter 6, hurricanes are very destructive to life and property, particularly intense ones which sweep over low-lying coastlines. Many scientists believe that if the maximum wind speeds in hurricanes could be reduced, there would be a reduction of damage and loss of life. The view that hurricanes might be modified by seeding them with ice nuclei was first advanced by the famous scientist Irving Langmuir who performed the first test in 1947. Although there has been much interest in this subject since about 1960, only about half a dozen hurricane seeding tests have been conducted.

The most satisfactory tests were carried out on August 18 and 20, 1969, when Hurricane Debbie was seeded by aircraft on Project Stormfury, a joint program of the National Oceanic and Atmospheric Administration and the U. S. Navy. As shown in Fig. 8-7, following both periods of seeding, the peak winds within the hurricane decreased substantially at the air-

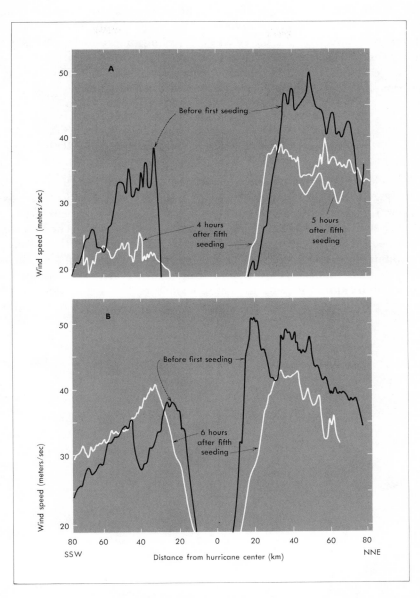

FIGURE 8–7 *Changes of wind speeds with time in Hurricane Debbie on (A) August 18, 1969 and (B) August 20, 1969. Winds were measured by an airplane flying at an altitude of 3,600 m along a track oriented from south-southwest to north-northeast. From R. C. Gentry, Science, 1970, **168**: 437–475. Copyright 1970 by the American Association for the Advancement of Science.*

Applications

129

craft flight level of about 3,600 m. Encouragingly, mathematical analyses have shown that ice-nuclei seeding of a hurricane outside the zone of maximum winds should cause a reduction of the peak speeds. These experimental and theoretical results have led to a feeling of cautious optimism that hurricanes can be weakened. There still are many uncertainties. It is considered essential that a few more experiments over the open oceans be performed, before seeding hurricanes about to strike populated areas.

Societal Consequences of Weather Modification

It is clear that we still have a great deal to learn about the science and technology of weather modification. It is becoming more evident that as we develop the knowledge and techniques to modify clouds, precipitation, and storm systems, there will be many societal consequences. There have already been legal problems over such questions as who owns the clouds and precipitation. Many others can be expected to arise. Atmospheric scientists now recognize that the only rational approach to weather modification is one which includes the participation of ecologists, sociologists, legal experts, and the public at large. The goal should be to maximize the benefits for all society.

Appendix

Length

1 centimeter (cm) = 0.394 inches (in)
1 meter (m) = 3.280 feet (ft)
1 kilometer (km) = 0.6214 statute miles (stat. mi) = 0.5396 nautical mile (naut. mi)
1 micron (μ) = 10^{-6} m = 10^{-4} cm = 3.94×10^{-5} in.

Velocity

1 m sec^{-1} = 3.6 km hr^{-1} = 2.24 mi hr^{-1} = 1.94 knots (kt)
1 knot = 1 naut. mi hr^{-1} = 1.15 mi hr^{-1} = 0.51 m sec = 1.85 km hr^{-1}

Mass

1 gram (g) = 0.0352 ounces (oz) = 0.00220 pounds (lb)
1 kilogram (kg) = 1,000 g
1 metric ton = 1,000 kg = 1.102 short tons = 2,205 lb

Pressure

1 millibar (mb) = 0.0145 lb in^{-2} = 0.750 millimeters of mercury (mm Hg) = 10^3 dynes cm^{-2}
1 standard atmosphere = 1013.2 mb = 14.69 lb in^{-2} = 760 mm Hg

Energy

15°C gram-calorie (cal) = 4.186 absolute joules (abs. joules) = 4.186×10^7 ergs = 1.16×10^{-6} kilowatt-hr (kw-hr) = 3.97×10^{-3} British thermal units (Btu)

Power

1 absolute watt (abs. watt) = 1 abs joule sec^{-1} = 0.239 cal sec^{-1} = 0.0569 Btu min^{-1} = 0.00134 electrical horsepower

Some properties of the Earth

Mass of the Earth $= 5.98 \times 10^{27}$ g

Mass of the oceans $= 1.32 \times 10^{24}$ g

Mass of the Earth's atmosphere $= 5.29 \times 10^{21}$ g

Mean radius of the Earth $= 6,371$ km

Mean gravitational acceleration at Earth's surface $= 980.7$ cm sec^{-2}

Suggestions for further reading

Barry, R. G., and R. J. Chorley, 1970, *Atmosphere, Weather, and Climate.* New York: Holt, Rinehart & Winston.

Battan, L. J., 1961, *The Nature of Violent Storms,* Garden City: Doubleday.

Battan, L. J., 1962, *Cloud Physics and Cloud Seeding.* Garden City: Doubleday.

Battan, L. J., 1962, *Radar Observes the Weather.* Garden City: Doubleday.

Battan, L. J., 1966, *The Unclean Sky.* Garden City: Doubleday.

Battan, L. J., 1969, *Harvesting the Clouds: Advances in Weather Modification.* Garden City: Doubleday.

Cole, F. W., 1970, *Introduction to Meteorology.* New York: Wiley.

Craig, R. A., 1968, *The Edge of Space.* Garden City: Doubleday.

*Craig, R. A., 1965, *The Upper Atmosphere.* New York: Academic Press.

Goody, R. M., and J. C. G. Walker, 1972, *Atmospheres.* Englewood Cliffs, N. J.: Prentice-Hall.

Hidy, G. M., 1967, *The Winds.* Princeton: Von Nostrand.

*Holton, J. R., 1972, *An Introduction to Dynamic Meteorology.* New York: Academic.

*Kraus, E. B., 1972, *Atmosphere-Ocean Interaction.* London: Clarendon Press.

Longley, R. W., 1970, *Elements of Meteorology.* New York: Wiley.

Lorenz, E. N., "The Circulation of the Atmosphere," *American Scientist,* Vol. 54, No. 4 (December 1966), 402–420.

Ludlam, F. G., and R. Scorer, 1957, *Cloud Study.* London: John Murray.

Mason, B. J., 1962, *Clouds, Rain and Rainmaking.* London: Cambridge University Press.

*Mason, B. J., 1971, *The Physics of Clouds.* (2nd Ed.) London: Oxford University Press.

Ohring, G., 1966, *Weather on the Planets.* Garden City: Doubleday.

Riehl, H., 1972, *Introduction to the Atmosphere.* (2nd Ed.) New York: McGraw-Hill.

Scorer, R., 1972, *Clouds of the World.* Harrisburg, Pa.: Stackpole Books.

*Sellers, W. D., 1965, *Physical Climatology.* Chicago: University of Chicago Press.

Sutcliffe, R. C., 1966, *Weather and Climate.* New York: W. W. Norton.

Sutton, O. G., 1962, *The Challenge of the Atmosphere.* London: Harper.

Tricker, R. A. R., 1970, *An Introduction to Meteorological Optics.* New York: American Elsevier Publishing.

*Uman, M. A., 1969, *Lightning.* New York: McGraw-Hill.

Uman, M. A., 1971, *Understanding Lightning.* Carnegie, Pa.: Bek Technical Publications.

Wilson, C. L. (Director), 1972, *Inadvertent Climate Modification: Report of the Study of Man's Impact on Climate (SMIC).* Cambridge, Mass.: M.I.T. Press.

*For advanced treatments of the subjects involved.

Index